[untitled]

issue nine

First published by Pinion Press 2021

Copyright © 2021 Remains with individual authors

ISBN 978-1-922465-66-5

ISSN 1832 5416

This book is copyright. Apart from any fair dealing for the purposes of study, research, criticism, review, or as otherwise permitted under the Copyright Act, no part may be reproduced by any process without written permission. Enquiries should be made through the publisher.

This is a work of fiction. Any similarities between places and characters are a coincidence.

Editorial committee: Adelle Xue, Anna Bilbrough, Emily Whitehead, Emma Fuelling, Erin Lyon, Joey To, Josephine Hong, Katrina Burge, Meg Hellyer, Michaela Harden, Sam Stevens, Scott Vandervalk

Cover image: Kev Howlett (inspired by *Beatrice & Turkey*)
Layout and typesetting: Busybird Publishing

Pinion Press
2/118 Para Road
Montmorency, Victoria
Australia 3094

Pinion Press is an imprint of Busybird Publishing

Back copies of *[untitled]* can be found on the website:
www.busybird.com.au

Contents

Editorial	1
Beatrice & Turkey *CJ Quince*	3
Ventilating *Andrew Nest*	22
I Just Said It *Samuel Elliot*	30
Winter *Kate Welsh*	54
It's Judgement Day, Bitch! *Beau Windon*	62
Life Happens When *Erin McWhinney*	69
Short Story Competition	**73**
Fever *Rebecca Howden*	76
Vetiver *Zachary Pryor*	96
If You Are But a Dream *James Karantonis*	119
Marissa's Present *Dominique Davidson*	138

Hindsight *Danielle Hughes*	149
Elephant and Wheelbarrow *Linda Kemp*	164
Love Looks Like *Laura Pettenuzzo*	180
Body Bags *Mark Phillips*	191
Fire Trap *Melanie Hutchinson*	205
Distorted *Jamisyn Gleeson*	216
Becoming Cat *Jessica L Wilkinson*	224
The Enemy *Odette Des Forges*	228
With & Without *Justine Stella*	240
LBD Widow *Zhiling Gao*	253
Author Bios	257

Editorial

I feel I should talk about pivoting here. Or being unprecedented. They are the Hot™ terms of 2020. Pivoting business, pivoting lifestyle, pivoting personalities. Unprecedented times, unprecedented circumstances, unprecedented number of Zoom meetings, etc…

But we are in 2021 and if I hear these two words one more time I'll either do something drastic or crawl into the weeping corner to weep. Yes I have a weeping corner. What other option did I have after being confined to my apartment for 112 days?

In all seriousness, it's been a rough year, what with fires and viruses and lockdowns and other calamities. Everyone's had to adapt in some way or another, and anxieties have run rife through many communities.

I think those anxieties are reflected in stories of *[untitled]* this year. But more importantly, the stories of *[untitled]* reflect the things that got us through the monster that was 2020. Bravery, humour, love, murder... hm, one of those things is not like the others.

Anyway, I think this year's *[untitled]* also reflects the fact that the importance of storytelling has not changed; not for us and not for the world. There is a reason reading levels went up over 2020. Last year reminded us that we tell and read stories to find an escape, to make others feel better, to feel better ourselves, and just to expel all of that positive and negative baggage out into the world.

These are some good stories that have come out of 2020, and I hope you, dear reader, enjoy the little individual sparks of hope they contain as much as we did.

Read on!

Michaela Harden
Publishing Intern

Beatrice & Turkey

CJ Quince

The dust settled as the dunny cart pulled away from the house, its essential service having made short work of the past few days' unmentionables. Beatrice mumbled to herself and adjusted her thick glasses swinging surreptitiously from frayed string. Her back ached, she resented it (her back *and* the pain), and they resented her as she fumbled up the once blue, now faded grey stairs with a sack of potatoes. The house stood halfway up a typical hill in the Brisbane suburbs, mongrel things to get up with your pushbike on a hot summer's day. The price of trudging upstairs a half-dozen times a day was paid back by a high set house, enabling the breeze to bring some hearty relief.

Beatrice struggled to the kitchen and began to unload the potatoes into the bottom of the pantry at the back of the room, the coolest place in the house. This gave them a fighting chance of surviving for subsequent meals and avoiding having a sprout. Since the boys had left home and only her and Frank were catered for, it was a challenge to get through the food. The thought of cooking less was one that occasionally entered her mind. After two years of concerned empty nesting, it was still yet to coalesce.

Using a tea towel tied to the waist of her frayed floral house dress to mop the sweat off her gradually wrinkling forehead, Beatrice thought, and not for the first time, how much she would love to have one of them electric fans plugged in. Her and Frank only had electricity connected a few years ago and a telephone in the past six months (good for talking to the boys now that they'd married out). Some of Beatrice and Frank's friends had fans – a good excuse to visit them on a stinker of a day – but for now, she slid the narrow kitchen window up all the way and hoped the breeze would offer some relief.

The sack of potatoes was now empty, bar three large dusty pearls. Extracting them and placing the hessian sack by the bin, she began to peel, wash and cut them to prepare for supper. It was still only three in the afternoon, but it seemed as good a time as any, rather than slaving away after Frank returned from work.

Beatrice was nearly finished with the spuds when she heard a noise, a fast flutter of commotion by the window. She turned and gasped, emitting a cry of protest and denial.

A great big black bush turkey, red head and neck with yellow trimmings and a face built to antagonise, sat at the window ledge and peered in. With the window open there was nothing to stop the Turkey dropping in and causing a ruckus.

'Don't you dare,' she said, threatening the bird with the large knife in her left hand; the glint of steel was tarnished and tempered by the impact of the potatoes.

The Turkey looked around, paying her little attention. It crouched down and looked like it was either settling in to roost and leer, or take a giant leap. Either outcome was unsatisfactory to Beatrice who had begun to cautiously encroach.

The Turkey seemed to give its attention then, yet was seemingly not alarmed. A fleeting thought of having turkey for dinner entered Beatrice's mind, but she dismissed it on two fairly significant accounts. One, there wasn't much meat on a bush turkey – she couldn't imagine why the Yanks ate them for giving thanks quite frankly. The second, was that the notion of slaughtering the creature became a spot more difficult when, with one more step, she tripped an invisible line of personal poultry space and the animal leapt into the kitchen. It gobbled and guffawed as it ran across the linoleum.

'No!' Beatrice chased the animal around the small room. This act seemed only to aggravate the animal (and the aggrieved human occupant) and its wings fluttered and spewed a few black feathers that floated through the air.

It was a tired effort that left her panting and stressed, but Beatrice was able to herd the thing to the front door and heft it out onto the verandah. With great relief, for both parties, it gobbled and ran towards the bushland that met the back fence behind the shed, passing the chook house. Ignoring the cries of its cousins, it flapped over the fence and left the scene in haste.

'How is it that we can live in a city, yet the bush animals live in our backyard?' Beatrice bellowed at Frank as he waddled slowly up the front stairs. His half-smile disappeared as any hope of a pleasant greeting left his pasty half-bald, very round and shining head.

'What are you talking about, Bee?' he panted, his shirt sticking to his back, the smell of tanning oil and hard, wholesome work following him. There was no embrace offered nor desired from either party.

'Flamin' turkey came into the kitchen. Nearly had a heart attack chasing it out.'

'Blimey,' he said. He took off his shoes and wandered inside. 'Geesh, it's hot in here.'

'I had to close everything up so I didn't get invaded again.'

'Well, maybe I can rig something up on the weekend,' Frank offered as he grabbed a tall boy of beer from the fridge and extracted a glass from the overhead cupboard. He opened the kitchen window, sat down and poured himself a glass that was emptied in moments with a measured gasp of relief.

'That thing comes back, you're in charge of chasing it this time.' Beatrice gestured at the window.

'Yes dear, I doubt you'll see it again, you would have given it a fright.'

She turned the stove on forcefully to boil the potatoes. The sun was setting now, but would still torment the couple for another two hours as the summer solstice berated them.

'What's for supper, darling?'

'Was nearly some darn turkey, but you'll have to settle for chook.'

'Oh,' Frank said with some relief. 'Probably for the best.'

The next day, a Tuesday, Frank took off to work before seven. He clumsily swung his stumpy leg over the seat of the rusted pushbike and wheezed as it squeaked down the hill towards the tannery, his place of work these past two decades and counting.

Beatrice busied herself around the house and by midday was sitting, reading a gossip magazine (only to do the crosswords, naturally) with a spot of dinner, stopping occasionally to slay a fly with the corpse-encrusted swatter. She chewed on the bland white bread extracted from the bread bin, a few slices of tomato, a piece of cooked chicken meat from last night's supper and a thick, crispy piece of iceberg lettuce with salt and pepper that careened down and covered the feast.

The day was not quite as hot as the previous, but the thick cover of clouds made it muggy. The thick air had already seeped into the kitchen and was slung onto Beatrice's shoulders.

She'd just had the butter-covered bread and was one bite into the lettuce leaf when a ruffling of feathers turned her permed head, iceberg flapping, still hanging from her mouth.

'You,' Beatrice growled around her food. The Turkey looked at her with intense indifference. Lessons had been learnt, and the window was half-closed. There was room enough at the bottom for the bird to stick its head through as if to say 'peek-a-boo' but would otherwise go no further. The front door, however, was open.

Slowly, as if in a standoff from one of those Yankee-Italian Western pictures, Beatrice stood, spat the lettuce back on the table and sidestepped with extreme caution out of the kitchen in the direction of the front, passing the Turkey at the window as she went. The bird made no attempt to follow, and within moments Beatrice was in reaching distance of the front door. With glee, she leapt at it and latched it closed; the house was secured. She returned triumphant to the kitchen, her smirk sliding off her face as the Turkey stood, nonchalant, as turkeys do, on the kitchen table, a piece of chicken in its mouth.

Beatrice, shocked and angered, in that order, looked at the window with anguish – it was still half-closed.

'How the devil?' The bird offered no response, rather devouring its prized morsel instead.

'You thieving cannibal!' she shrieked and grabbed a knife off the kitchen counter and spent the next harrowing fifteen minutes chasing her home invader around the house. Finally, panting, sweating and parched, Beatrice forced it into the living room with all exits blocked. She contemplated murder but thought of the already stained carpet and the cost of replacing it and decided instead on opening the main door and coercing the creature into the freedom of the outdoors instead.

With the door closed, the searing afternoon was spent cleaning the mess: a few feathers, some household items dislodged from their usual pre-eminent locations, and the removal of some unmentionable presents left by the intruder.

Supper was prepared and, as Frank huffed and puffed up the stairs, he was to show no signs of disappointment or displeasure at missing out on a pleasant greeting for the second day in a row.

'You need to fix something, or I'll fix you,' Beatrice said as she explained the day's events. She huffed and sat down to eat, now hot and exhausted. Frank sniffed the main dish, pork, with some reservations.

'Where's the gravy?'

'No flamin' time, lord muck,' she bit back.

'What's that taste?' he asked, mildly aware of the fire emanating from his soulmate.

'I fried it with garlic, thought I'd try something different,' Beatrice replied with somewhat less venom.

'So *that's* garlic?' His furry off-white eyebrows shot up as he took a bite.

'What do you think?' Beatrice asked, still too tired as yet to try it herself.

'Nice,' he said as he sipped his beer, slow to return for more and not making eye contact. 'Could we have the gravy next time?'

Wednesday morning, the wheezing and squeaking of Frank had subsided over the dusty road and Beatrice's day began with some resolute determination. The usual chores were completed early, the sun shone and brought fresh heat into the house, and the kitchen window was in its most upper position, permitting a scant breeze into the narrow room. By midday, once again, Beatrice had completed her tasks and was sitting down to a dinner of similar constitution to the day prior. The last of the chicken meat was sitting atop her plate, tempting her, but she ate around it whilst casting a suspicious eye to the open window.

She crunched the lettuce slowly, and before long her food was gone, except for the chicken. With a sigh she stood up, ignoring the flies that flew and buzzed, and she walked to the sink where she took the fresh chicken meat that she'd left to defrost and put it into the fridge. Heaving the heavy door and closing it a moment later with a bang did little to cover the now familiar sound of soon to be ruffled feathers.

The Turkey was, predictably, sitting atop the sill and at full height, with no lowered timber to narrow its entry port.

'Well, hello,' Beatrice smiled, 'nice to see you again,' and without ceremony she shuffled towards the living room, checking to confirm that the opposite door to the hallway was closed, then slid the wooden kitchen door gently, groaning as it went on its rails. Beatrice smiled again as she listened to the noise of the bird entering the kitchen and tiptoeing across the laminex kitchen table. Shooting outside quietly, she was at the window in moments and drew it closed with a shrewd 'gotcha!' to accompany it.

Skipping with glee, she returned to the kitchen door and listened: the Turkey was seemingly unperturbed and was tapping around, now apparently on the kitchen floor.

'Better not mess up my floor,' she whispered. Next to the door sat a white wooden bookcase with memories enshrined in glass leaning at an acute angle atop it. Glinting there was an axe, freshly sharpened. Frank had refused to rig up anything of use until the weekend.

Lifting the weapon, the blade made a *ding* as it brushed against the doily atop the bookcase. With a sneer and a steady moment to prepare, Beatrice slid open the door with a hurry and a hurrah.

Her triumph was premature: the Turkey had gobbled the chicken on her plate and now guffawed as it flew up into the air, missing the swing of an indecisive blade, and escaped the kitchen over Beatrice's baffled head.

She tore after the animal with a grunt of displeasure and was on the verge of another strike when it took off and wound through the house out the back window, curtains whipping in every direction.

'Flamin' poor excuse for a piece of poultry, be darned with ya!' she yelled ineffectually. The spare room had not been secured – she hadn't thought it necessary to check the whole house.

Frank huffed and puffed up the stairs as the sun began its slow and unrelenting retreat. He recalled, as he neared the entrance to the house, that when it was time to 'speak' to the chooks about the lack of fresh eggs he would often leave the axe by their lair to give them some productive motivation. Now, he noticed the axe by the front door, glinting and sharp yet devoid of blood. With the hint of a message received, he began to tiptoe into the house but made it no more than three abridged strides when a growl could be heard from the direction of the kitchen. It was louder than the boiling water and clanging of plates and, turning to the noise, he saw a sight most frightening.

'Hello dear,' he said with forced cheer, 'what's for supper?'

Thursday morning came and went – there was a bare sniff of rain in the air – but the clouds promised little as the midday meal was laid in a now familiar pattern. The leftover chook from the previous night was fresh and, since Beatrice was getting jealous of her adversary, she ate some of it first before allowing the remainder to stay on the table. The dishes were done, excepting the tempting platter of white meat, and still there was no sign of the enemy.

'Stupid animal could at least be punctual,' she muttered. After a half-hour of waiting, she huffed and gave up and decided to inspect the surrounds of the house.

The heat blasted her as she patrolled around the perimeter of the house. There were no signs of the bird on a second tour. Beatrice's foggy eyes, however, noticed some damage to the chook wire on the coop. Looking around, there was predictably one stray layer, the rest were clucking and scratching without a hint of intelligence nor stress inside their shaded home. With minimum fuss, the animal was returned to its abode. Beatrice put on her glasses, and the fence was repaired in short order with a twist of the pliers.

Turning back to the house, Beatrice froze. Moving in a confident, one might say 'cocky' demeanour, the Turkey strutted past her, up the yard and with a quick flap it was over the fence and disappeared into the surrounding bushland. Beatrice was dumbfounded into a static position and also unarmed and unable to take advantage of the opportunity.

Shaking from her pose, she raced up the stairs and found, predictably, that the bait of the chicken was removed and the table had been further scratched. It was now beginning to look like the bottom of a budgie cage. The doors to the kitchen being closed meant that it had ventured no further into the house, and had seemingly grabbed its prize and departed, posthaste.

'Hello darling,' Frank said hours later upon his return, 'any luck today?'

'Not yet,' she said with a calm that surprised her husband, 'but tomorrow is a new day.'

Friday's midday meal was the same as the day before, yet Beatrice was now set, determined and ready to pounce. She wasn't going to leave the kitchen this time. The doors were closed, the window wide open and the scent of rain in the distance began to seep into the small, muggy and unpleasant room. She continued to sweat as her hands gently rubbed the barrel of Frank's gun. He said it was for hunting, but she never saw him use it for such. He'd brought it when he came home from the war. Beatrice suspected he'd taken it in lieu of payment for something, but as far as she knew the army never issued double-barrelled shotguns.

At any rate, the weapon had been cleaned (Frank at least took care of that on occasional weekends) and was loaded with two shells.

'Don't know why I hadn't thought of this before,' Beatrice muttered. The gun had been locked away of course, but the shells were sitting out, as usual, downstairs near the laundry and became the prompt for her new plan.

An hour passed and the sweltering continued and Beatrice began to nod off in the heat. The smell of chicken and vegetable scraps invaded her nose and jolted her awake from time to time.

Eventually, there was a flutter and Beatrice came alive with a stiffening of the spine.

'Well, well,' she whispered as the barrels slowly came up to face the animal. The Turkey sat on its perch on the windowsill and seemed to pay her no mind. The head moved spasmodically as it surveyed the room and hopped inside, making a few tentative steps towards its meal. The Turkey seemed unaware of the dual barrels that followed it and, as it neared the plate, it grabbed the prize with a snap, followed by the *click* of the arming of the unfamiliar black, shining piece.

The Turkey, as if suddenly awakened to an unpleasant and potentially mortal situation, shot a look at Beatrice and turned towards the window.

'Oh no you don't,' Beatrice said. But as she followed the animal her position slipped. Her sweaty thighs failed to adhere to the plastic-coated chair. She slid off her throne of belligerence, the barrel raised high and gave a salute with a thunderous applause as a shell ignited, shattered and slammed into the ceiling above. A confetti-like shower of housing descended, a celebration of another successful meal (for the Turkey).

Only a moment had passed and surprise at the damage caused had been brushed aside like so many fragments in a rapidly greying perm. The Turkey had returned to the windowsill and was ready to leap to freedom, but stopped for a critical second to turn its head and see how the less than compliant giver of feasts was positioned. That was all Beatrice needed, and this time she didn't slip.

The second shot rang out over the neighbourhood.

The police arrived after a time, and the gun and shells were confiscated after they were content that no human was at risk (except perhaps the sole occupant of the house). This seemed a fair assessment when looking at the hole in the kitchen ceiling, but the mystery remained as to the identity of the intended victim.

The story of an invading bush animal was believed, but no body could be found. To this, Beatrice was intensely confused. She'd hit the flamin' animal: it had fallen from its perch with a pathetic squawk. But by the time she tore outside, keen to celebrate her belated victory, it was nowhere in sight.

The lead officer took a look at the spare shells and chuckled.

'Well, this might explain it,' he said, holding aloft one of the articles. 'See these marks?' He pointed to the shell. There were tiny marks all over the darn thing. 'Someone's been tinkering with these.'

Beatrice frowned. 'Whatdayamean tinkerin'?'

'Tiny holes have been pecked in there,' he added.

'Pecked?'

'Just a figure of speech,' he said after realising the revelations that his comment irradiated, 'and some moisture got in, quite a lot in fact. The powder was damp. I'm surprised they would have fired at all, frankly.'

'Evidently they did,' Beatrice said as she looked up at the kitchen ceiling.

'Aye,' he said, 'but you don't need much oomph to knock a bit of ceiling out. To kill something, even a bird at that range, you need a functioning weapon, otherwise you'll just wing it.' He smiled and shrugged, and then they were gone.

The storm hit just as the day began to head towards a close.

'Hello darling, what the—?' Frank's half-smile slipped from his round head as he entered the kitchen huffing and heaving. Beatrice was sitting down, looking at him. Inexplicably, she began to laugh.

Frank broke out into a broad grin. Her joy was infectious.

'Why are you laughing?' she said, sucking in air, barely enough to expel the words.

'I have no idea, why are you?'

But she couldn't answer. She recalled the fact that on Wednesday all the windows were closed – the ones up the back of the house were *always* fastened. And that Thursday, the chook pen had been damaged at just the right time to cause an opportune distraction. And that the shells had been left out, as was typical, but *were* in a good working fashion (for Frank always checked them when he cleaned the gun).

As time passed, there was no more talk of turkeys, nor any to be seen on their property. The ceiling was fixed by Frank, and a patch where the repairs were facilitated remained for decades as a reminder of that fateful day.

They never talked about that bush turkey again. Perhaps there was some kind of unspoken understanding, for Frank never once questioned his wife as to why she would leave a small piece of chicken on a plate just underneath the kitchen window every day at around midday. Nor would he ask as to its whereabouts when it would promptly and without ceremony disappear shortly thereafter.

He thought it was perhaps best to leave a tender moment alone.

Ventilating

Andrew Nest

'He's no better, no worse,' Ma tells me over WeChat.

'But he's still on the ventilator,' I confirm.

'Yes, but he will get better.'

I don't want to doubt my mother's optimism, but also can't ignore the probability that Ba, my father, a fifty-year-old man with an underlying lung condition, might die from the virus. Cutting through the red tape of lockdowns in two countries to see him would be complicated. But neither parent would have me disrupting my studies to be with them anyway.

I go back to my notes on the pathobiological processes of sickle cell anaemia, occlusion and dysfunction, the result of which deprives the body of vitality and cuts life expectancy by nearly thirty years…

Outside, the night creeps towards an unfamiliar, early stillness, excess traffic siphoned from the adjacent main road by decree. The residual vehicles swish by in drizzling rain. The occasional high-powered engine among them seems to simulate the groan of frustration in the city's asphyxiation. Night trams slice air along steel, both defying and enhancing the abnormality, staunchly loyal to their timetables, yet transporting mostly no one to dead ends and back, via city central, now like an abandoned theme park. 'Shop local' has taken on a different connotation. The supermarket across the road has assumed the status of a go-to oasis. But only provisionally. The invisible that lurks is the worry. Sharing the air with other masked warriors is a game of Russian roulette. Hoard and then hibernate in isolation. Alright for some.

I rub my forehead. Time for a break. I think about turning on the TV, but news of the virus transmits from those airwaves. I avoid it.

The adjacent park in the black of night is where I must head. It's become my haven despite the winter freeze. As I run, I clear my lungs of phlegm, a symptom of bronchiectasis, the same genetic condition as my father's.

The next stage of the internship is upon me. Eight weeks in emergency medical care, work that will involve managing coronavirus cases in a critical care unit, playing the role of possible sacrificial lamb as well as saviour. This is where having strong maths and science skills, filial duty, a grandfather who was a doctor, and an interest in my own medical condition has got me. But in the context of the pandemic and my inflamed bronchial tubes, I perhaps shouldn't have been afforded the investment the government has put in me. Yet here I am: reluctant martyr for the cause.

I'm screened at the entrance to the hospital like I'm entering a radiation zone. Masked team members welcome me with elbow bumps and eyes that I can only imagine mean smiles. We stand apart, brothers and sisters at arm's length, the word 'huddle' a misnomer. The clinical supervisor informs us of an increased Covid caseload. We armour up.

I accompany a nurse on pre-rounds trying to make sense of imagings and charts I've been given.

The first patient I see is Archie, an eighty-one-year-old man, who tells me that his great-grandfather died young during the 1918 flu pandemic.

'I don't like my chances,' he says, heaving breaths. I reassure him that care is better now. There's a ban on family visitations in the critical care ward, so I've been asked if I can facilitate a video call between

Archie and other family members. He waves limply in response to the intimate pleas and well-wishes from kin. How long should I allow them to see him clinging to life's cliff? I block out my own family worries by counting. After six minutes, I play the cruel executioner of time; there are others to attend to.

Edith, eighty-seven, has an underlying heart disease as well as the virus. The ICU room hosts a family of 5-star machinery, the high-cost, sterilised price of life. Seeing the frail woman so helpless stirs my sense of compassion. Years of medical school boils down to doing our best to save her. As a team, we shift her onto her stomach, but it seems to increase distress. She needs intubation. Mask ventilation first. I watch the set-up procedure. The patient has fluid in the airway. The doctor has trouble guiding the laryngoscope. A new blade is attached to the device. While the respiratory therapist adjusts the patient's head position, I'm asked to press down on the larynx to help bring the vocal cords into view. A splutter has our heads drawing back while we keep our hands in position. I hold my breath. The RT wipes sputum from the patient's mouth. I pray my mask and shield are doing their jobs; heavy particle transmission might kill anyone. We get it right, and the tube is finally attached to the ventilator. A nurse and a pharmacist confer with the doctor on sedation and pain control. We leave Edith to manage on her own.

Back home, I make the nightly call to my mother. 'There's no change' is all she can tell me about Ba's condition.

The next day, the workload intensifies, yet some in my team convey an upbeat manner, injecting humour. Is their buoyancy natural or a contrivance, a coping strategy? Or maybe they just don't carry too much emotional baggage. I then realise that verbal expression, voice and hand gesture need to step up when facial expression is smothered by an oral straitjacket. I wish I could muster some of the same positive energy. Instead, I peruse vital stats, tick charts, go over protocols, write notes and double-check everything, anaesthetising myself from any human feelings.

After pre-rounds, I do rounds with the physician and see a repeat of the tug of war between machine and the grim reaper.

A team member comes down with cold symptoms. I'm asked if I can work an extra double shift. It's all part of work conditions.

Healthcare workers in the state are contracting the infection in larger numbers. I conjure up an image of hospitals as big aerosol cans of viral matter. Do we need to be even more careful about distancing and removing our armour? Perhaps we should all be wearing full body suits, with a backpack inside, in which we store our daily sustenance and eat within the suits on our meal breaks. The PPE we chuck out after one use is also symptomatic of a sick society. Where's all that waste going? I suddenly cough. Such an involuntary reflex has aroused quite some suspicion lately.

I begin to wonder about the right balance between pricey overtreatment of patients and therapeutic nihilism. The economic fallout from Covid will affect the young the most. How much should their futures be compromised in order to prevent death among the elderly and infirm? Is the ultimate goal of medicine to continually find cures and vaccines in order to prolong life? On the other hand, in addition to obvious compassionate reasons, isn't investment in life-saving treatment the reward elderly loved ones deserve for the progress they have contributed to?

Leaving the hospital, I hear a caller on talkback radio complaining about the 'lax' attitude of the staff in the nursing home where the caller's mother is. '… and they're spreading it because they wear masks that don't fit …' Such generalisations do us no favours. What's the real evidence for the spreading? I inadvertently accelerate through a red light. A flash. I curse. How many hundred bucks is that?

Ba is still the same. I complete my routine: eat, study, run, shower, sleep.

The following day, more patients are brought in, together with more beds. My ICU patients increase to three. Edith has died. I'm told she was a former aged care facility manager and that no one was by her side. It was a miscarriage of honour for her as well as a torturous gasping struggle. And there's still the respiratory infection one of us might have picked up trying to save her. Expressing condolences to her family in person seems too brief and shameful.

'You're from China,' says my newest patient. 'The source of all this.'

I know to expect someone might have a go at my appearance for the contagion.

'Second-generation Australian,' I tell him.

'I can't picture it.'

The slur hurts, but I show restraint. 'My job is to save lives.'

'Yeah.'

It's not a concession that takes the edge off the insult. 'Fair go, mate,' I should have said. He's in his forties and will likely survive.

'Maybe you'd prefer a robot one day,' I quip.

'Now, there's an idea.'

He then tells me that his father died of the virus. So the guy's going through stuff too. Finding someone rightly or wrongly to blame is his way of coping. Maybe it *should be* a robot doing this job. Would that be a good thing or not? What if it's made in China?

I'm exhausted after the double shift, but there's still another one. I'll need more than a two-day break afterwards.

Ma doesn't answer the call at the usual time. I make repeated attempts, fearing the worst. My appetite has suddenly gone. I can't just sit and wait. Nor can I concentrate on study. I change into my running clothes and head out into the midnight hour, breaching the curfew that's now in place.

I reach the small reserve in less than a minute, stealing oxygen like a fugitive running for his life. The path is barely visible but I know my footing. Ten fifty-metre sprints is the plan. I focus on my breathing as well as my step. After an exhaustive final rep, I cry out into the night for my father … I need my ventilator, too.

I Just Said It

Samuel Elliot

'You've been avoiding me,' Malcolm told Lindsay as they lurched along the foreshore area around Drummoyne cove.

'Rubbish,' Lindsay said. The sway he'd developed had become much more pronounced since they'd left the pub.

Malcolm had ensured he stuffed Lindsay full of alcohol, ordering him beer after beer. Not that he needed it. He wasn't used to putting them away like that. Marion, Lindsay's wife, was the seasoned drinker. Lindsay drank like an expectant mother.

'It's true.' Malcolm gave Lindsay a little nudge with his shoulder and nearly sent him toppling off the edge of the path to crash into the high-tide waves below.

'Steady on,' Lindsay slurred.

'*You* steady on.'

'You've bloody got me pissed.' Lindsay was struggling to stuff his pipe, hampered by gusts of winds kicked up by the bay.

'You're just getting clumsy in your advancing years,' Malcolm said in jest.

'Always was.' Lindsay raised his hands to Malcolm, turning them back and forth while regarding them with comically widened eyes. 'Christ! When did some joker replace my hands with an old man's ones?'

Malcolm looked at them too, more flatteringly. How gnarled and stubby each finger was, denoting that they'd been badly broken countless times.

'These things are magnets for a hammer,' Lindsay told him. 'I guess I'm divinely blessed that I've still got all of them intact. Should've probably lost a couple, with all the bone-headed things I've done over the years.'

Malcolm didn't respond, kept peering at Lindsay's wriggling fingers, as they turned back and forward. How scarred the flesh was, how calloused.

They were almost the roughest hands that Malcolm had ever felt, losing out by a whisker to

Barry, his father. Lindsay's hands never caused discomfort when they were on Malcolm's body, wherever they roamed and found themselves, caressed, tickled, scrunched, bunched. They felt infinitely nicer than any of the others Malcolm had ever encountered, be they the fumbling and clammy ones of fellow youths, snatching moments in makeshift sanctuaries tucked away from the notice and disgust of the public, or the more deft and smooth ones, found in Paris and the rest of his travels.

Lindsay's were the best by far, and he'd only encountered them last, after all the others. The last and best and the best ones to last him for the rest of his life.

'Put your hands down,' Malcolm lightly smacked Lindsay's shoulder. 'What will people think?'

He nodded toward a young mother pushing along a pram. A young man walked next to her, with a little girl seated about his shoulders. All of them shuffled with that weariness found in those that had spent a big day together. They acknowledged Malcolm and Lindsay with a nod and a smile and received the same in turn.

The young family no doubt assumed it was a father and his adult son out for a stroll. No one ever suspected the truth. Malcolm swung between feeling comforted by that and insulted, to be dismissed so, or to be assumed as something else, because the reality was too impossible to consider, much less countenance. Why couldn't they be viewed like any other couple, with the same level of acceptance, or better yet, disinterest?

'What's wrong with them?' Lindsay kept waving his hands around Malcolm, his pipe in his clenched teeth sputtering unlit tobacco.

'Nothing at all.' Malcolm yearned to add that he thought they were perfect and that he wanted nothing more than to take one in his own and that all that was stopping him from doing so was not the reaction of fellow members of the public, or the very real threat of police intervention and some criminal charges, but Lindsay's reaction.

Lindsay dropped his hands, removed his fedora and wiped at the sweat on his brow.

The summer of 1957 was proving to be as scorching hot as its predecessor, with the early night loath to relinquish the oppressive heat established by the day.

'Where you taking us?' Lindsay asked.

'Don't recognise this place?' Malcolm swung his hand over the sprawling park adjacent to the path.

'Sisters Crescent Park?' Lindsay stifled a belch in his fist.

'Used to be called that.' Malcolm veered sharply, crossing the road after an ancient Coupe trundled past and left a pong of diesel fumes. 'It's been called Brett Park for a while now.'

So many weekends had been spent roaming its expanse. Sometimes everyone else had been indisposed, and it would just be Lindsay and him, doing precious little except spending time together.

Malcolm turned and beckoned to Lindsay.

Lindsay wiped at his face again. His face so sweaty and crimson, distant and pensive. Maybe he'd got Lindsay too drunk, perhaps now was not the time to present his proposition. The proposition that he'd been kicking around and perfecting for a long, long while now. Maybe he should leave it unsaid, never to be said. Perhaps it was best to just continue on as they were, with the world remaining ignorant to them.

'You alright?' Malcolm said.

'Fine. Just got a bit lost on memory lane for a moment I guess.' Lindsay grinned his sheepish grin, that made him look twenty years younger.

'Righto then,' Malcolm pointed to the field stretched out before them. 'Remember when we used to play footy here?'

'I don't know if you could really call that footy, considering it was just us two.'

'Sorry, forget you were such a purist.'

'That's alright.' Lindsay winked at him. 'Just don't let it happen again.'

There was the humour, the innocent larrikin humour that proved that Lindsay and Barry were two peas in a pod, cut from the same cloth and all that. No wonder their mateship had lasted a lifetime and was still going strong, maybe even stronger than ever.

Malcolm sometimes considered what Barry would do if he found out about Lindsay and him. Would he accept him? Them?

Malcolm had never heard his father making vile remarks about men that way inclined before and he'd certainly been with his father around others making them in many a pub.

But Malcolm knew he'd most likely disown him. Even if he were accepting of the way Malcolm was, surely, he'd never accept it being with Lindsay. He'd never countenance the admittedly stark age difference, or the circumstances in which they'd met.

'Might need a sit down,' Lindsay ambled over to a nearby bench.

'Feeling your age a bit?' Malcolm trailed after Lindsay, but preferred to stand, chain-smoking.

'More feeling all those beers and that roast,' Lindsay patted his gut, which was no rival to Barry's.

'Maybe I'm feeling my age a bit too though. It's not a crime is it?'

He never shied away from the topic of getting older or losing his looks, which made Malcolm swoon more. If Lindsay wasn't precious about his handsomeness waning, maybe then he'd be more inclined to take seriously Malcolm's proposition.

If nothing was taken too seriously, anything could be seriously considered. Surely.

'They do a right good roast at that joint.' Lindsay picked at his teeth. 'I'll have to take Marion there one of these days. She doesn't love a feed as much as a drink, but she still loves one. Or tolerates one in exchange for the other.'

He chuckled lightly and his eyes glazed over.

Jealousy flushed in Malcolm and it was hot enough to rival whatever the sun was still toasting his shoulders and the backs of his bare arms with. 'You really love her, don't you?'

That snapped Lindsay out of it, fixed his gaze straight on Malcolm. 'Course I do.'

'And me?'

'I dunno.' Lindsay cracked a grin, there was something that had once belonged to a pig wedged in between two of his large teeth. 'Do you love her or what?'

'I meant me and you and you know it.' Malcolm's

voice had risen, become effete, he cleared his throat like that would deepen it, would quell his frayed nerves too.

'What about you?' Lindsay dug out whatever it was in his teeth and ate it.

'Do you love me?' Malcolm ceased his pacing and turned to face Lindsay head-on, bracing as if he were in the path of a locomotion.

Confoundment passed across Lindsay's face, before it set in stoicism. 'What's all this?'

'Answer.'

'Settle alright.' Lindsay's eyes cleared, all jocular drunkenness had vanished. 'Course I do. I bloody love you.'

And that word of love surmised only that belonging to a mate for another mate, platonic mateship, a blokey bonding but nothing more. One you'd use to express your happiness that you had a person to socialise with, escape the house and the missus for a while with, a fellow you'd sink a cheeky few with, nothing more.

Malcolm had prepared himself, rehearsed for every reaction and response, but all that went out the window in the moment he was met with what he considered the worst possible one.

His dumb instincts took over and he fell to his knees and hobbled towards a nonplussed Lindsay.

Lindsay smirked. 'You'll get mud all over them fancy pants of yours doing that.'

Malcolm reached out for him, hoping that some physical contact might put an end to Lindsay's joking.

'Christ mate.' Lindsay raised his hands to ward him off. 'Why you carrying on?'

'Don't call me mate,' Malcolm snapped, hurt by how panicked Lindsay had become, by how seriously he was trying to block his embrace. 'You know I'm more than that.'

'Shut it with that nonsense.' Lindsay smacked one of Malcolm's hands away and looked in every direction. No one was around. Only him and his shame. And Malcolm.

'Nonsense?' Malcolm repeated, even louder. So much for the plan.

'Yeah, that.' Lindsay shifted on the bench, slid toward the vacant side. Malcolm let his hands drop lamely to his side and gave no chase. Mounting outrage was all that was propping him up.

'I'll tell you what's nonsense.' Malcolm stood up again, stomped around.

'Calm down,' Lindsay said.

'The way this had been going on was nonsense, the denial, the act, the sneaking around and for years. For years now. And you can't even say you love me?'

Lindsay rose now too and approached Malcolm. Malcolm could tell by the way he carried himself, and the fretful glances he flung around, that it was not because he wanted to console him with closeness, but just to be near him so that he could reduce the risk of being overheard.

'I just said it,' Lindsay said and sure enough it was a whisper and sure enough he immediately checked over his shoulder to confirm Marion, or a policeman, or God, was not standing there.

'That wasn't what that was.' Malcolm took a step back, detesting how Lindsay was feebly trying to pander to him. To give just enough so that he wouldn't become too much. 'What you just said was just words. Words without meaning, you recited them. You did it exactly like children in my class repeat their times tables. They are a reflex for them, that has no meaning or importance attached, they aren't even formed in the brain. Just from the lungs. Recitation.' Malcolm's vision was blurred and he wiped at his face, hoping that it was just sweat and not tears. 'And even then, they only bother reciting the words because they are afraid of the strap. Not that I ever use it. But the fear is always there. The fear of not just saying something and what that can lead to. For them it might be the strap. What's the consequence that's got you so scared if you don't say what you're supposed to? It can't be the strap.'

He barked a mirthless laugh. 'And it sure can't be worried about hurting my feelings. So, what is it?'

Lindsay's brow furrowed. 'What are you honestly on about?'

'Do you remember when the first time I kissed you?'

Lindsay made to retreat and look around at the same time, but Malcolm shot forward and grabbed his face with both hands. 'Do you or not?'

He expected Lindsay to overpower him, to shove him off and launch him halfway across the park. But he made no move to retreat, or pry away Malcolm's hands either. He just stared fixedly at him, as if Malcolm were either a mirror, or a puzzle.

The silence between them was more stifling than the still-humid near-night.

'Do you or not?' Malcolm prompted.

'Yeah.'

'Tell me then.' He caressed one of Lindsay's earlobes to see if he'd tell him to stop. Lindsay turned his head by way of stopping him, but Malcolm thought it was because he was ticklish, not because he wasn't enjoying the contact.

Or he hadn't noticed.

He hadn't noticed that they were being intimate and affectionate as only lovers, the most besotted of lovers, could and would be like. Right here, in the heartland of Drummoyne, the suburb they'd spent most of their respective lives at, where the chances of being intruded upon were high, a fact no doubt constantly playing on Lindsay's mind and yet here he was, close to Malcolm, allowing Malcolm to rest his arms on his shoulders, his hands on his face. The perfection of their positioning, of the moment in general, struck Malcolm, left him giddy, and now it wasn't so much him tethering Lindsay to place to ensure he wouldn't flee, but Lindsay holding him upright so that he wouldn't tumble backward.

'Was right after you came back from your travels to gay Paree.' Lindsay mangled the city's pronunciation because he was trying to pronounce it like he knew Malcolm would.

That made Malcolm smile anew, he urged himself on, because otherwise that's all he would do, stand and smile and swoon. 'Go on.'

'Was in my kitchen, after a boozy day, Marion was out someplace. I was about as pissed as I'd ever been and couldn't open a stupid beer bottle, and you came up behind me. Put your head on my back. Rested your face there. Like it was, I dunno, a bed or a pillow or something. Something warm and comfortable. Not a bloody back.'

Malcolm remembered the kitchen. The proliferating shadows giving everything an ethereal quality, maybe more nightmare than pleasant dream.

The humidity of the newly-arrived night making everything measurable in levels of stickiness. The scent of spilled beer and some kind of cooking oil and something lemony that Marion must've used to clean. With a stubborn hint of some cloying perfume she favoured. The linoleum floor, gluing to Malcolm's bare feet, heralding his entry and approach toward Lindsay, as he hunched over the sink and fiddled and swore at the beer. The feel of Lindsay's flesh, so impossibly warm through the thin singlet and film of sweat he wore. The terrifying, exhilarating moment Malcolm had stretched out his arms around to hug him. How he thought that it would go on forever and he'd never actually get his arms around to their destination, linking up with one another.

But then it happened and they settled near Lindsay's navel and what he thought was unbearable anticipation and mounting dread a moment before was shown to be a mere triviality compared to the next one, of waiting for Lindsay's reaction as the words gushed out of Malcolm.

A confession of all his feelings that had started from when he was a teenager and only ever intensified over the following years. He'd taken himself off not just to explore the world and then spend an extended period to find himself or determine for sure if he was that way inclined because he knew, beyond a shadow of a doubt, that he was and had always been, but to see if he could strike up something with another man that could eventuate into something splendorous and sustaining. And he'd tried and he'd met many a great and kind and lovely man.

But they were not Lindsay and were never going to be, no matter how much he wished them so, or wished to extricate the all-consuming memory of Lindsay from his mind.

He had known that he needed to return home as soon as he was able and tell all to Lindsay, to hell with the consequences. Because it would be better to have Lindsay, his all, pummel him senseless and leave him in the dirt, than it would be to sit and ponder the possibilities in an uneven chair out the front of some bistro on the Champs-Élysées, with only a glass of sugared Absinthe to ward off the loneliness, the incompleteness, he had felt.

'I could feel you shaking,' Lindsay said. 'I thought about how I'd never known you to be scared before. Not over anything. And I remember thinking how I couldn't believe a human being could shake so much. It was like you were being electrocuted, or something. No joke.'

Malcolm gave a little chuckle, he wanted to bring Lindsay close, hug him, but he resisted. 'I thought you might beat me to a pulp, then chuck me out of your house. Maybe tell my parents too. Or maybe all of that.'

'How could you ever think that?' Lindsay's voice was soft, though clearly now with offense, not caution.

Malcolm forced a shrug. 'Just did.'

'All I was thinking about was how did you know that I was ...' Lindsay trailed off, looked down at his feet.

'That way inclined?'

A slow nod from Lindsay, but his eyes remained affixed downward. 'There'd been others. Here and there over the years. A few incidents after I'd married Marion. Quite a few slip-ups, if I'm being honest. Some blokes I used to work with, some blokes that worked for me. I stopped mucking around like that after this one time that this toe-rag tried blackmailing me.' Malcolm was torn between wanting to give assurance and clear up how lugubrious Lindsay looked and needing him to rid himself of whatever poison he'd carried around all these years. 'There was a couple of times where I went to a couple of places that you probably know about. I got a hiding at them, not always, but enough, and badly enough to make me never go back. Had to tell Marion and Barry I got into a pub-brawl.'

'Did Marion believe it?' Malcolm asked.

'Think so. But who really knows what anyone

thinks?' He sighed then and swayed. Malcolm suspected that it was not from any lingering effects of the multitude of beers, but from the taxing of his sharing. 'You've got to be careful if you're like us. There's so many sad, small people out there that wouldn't ever understand and wouldn't ever try to. They'd just rather beat you to death and string you up someplace.'

Malcolm stifled his joy at Lindsay referring to them together, but sat down before he fell down with the onrush of what that could mean. Lindsay took a seat too, but still kept a distance from Malcolm.

'Not everyone's like that and not everywhere is so oppressive,' Malcolm said. 'I know, I've been to them, we could go to one.'

'What was that?'

'Clear your ears out,' Malcolm said. 'I'm saying let's go. Let's leave. Bound for someplace far, far away.'

'Just up and leave? Like a gypsy caravan?'

'Why not?' Malcolm couldn't keep the excitement out of his voice when he saw that Lindsay was at least considering the prospect. 'Honestly why not? I know that you have the money to do it. You can set up a new business, you've obviously got the acumen to start somewhere and prosper.' He gave Lindsay's shoulder a little squeeze, couldn't help it. 'I'd get a glowing reference from my school, even if I left without giving notice. I'm sure of it. We could just go, just like that,' he snapped his fingers. 'And we really should.'

He'd unconsciously moved closer to Lindsay once again as he said this. Lindsay exhaled and sighed and pinched the bridge of his nose with thumb and forefinger, and the action was like it was pinching shut Malcolm's windpipe.

Malcolm waited and waited some more until he couldn't any longer. 'That's not the overwhelmingly receptive response I was aiming for.'

'I take it that Marion's not part of this grand plan?'

'Well, no.' Malcolm stammered.

'Then it's not happening.' Lindsay was resolute. 'I'm not leaving her. Not for anything. She's my wife and I love her.'

'You're living a lie.' Malcolm wanted to hurt Lindsay, or at least produce a crack in his veneer.

Lindsay smiled at him as if he were a pathetic little boy trying to backchat his father because he hadn't got his way. 'I'm really not mate. You've always been more into all of this stuff than I ever was. Besides, it'd never work. Never. No matter what magical faraway kingdom you had in mind.'

The casual air he said what he said, caused much more harm to Malcolm than if he just beat him to within an inch of his life. He felt his face twitch, but would rather have died than have himself reduced to tears in front of Lindsay.

'Being in love you mean?'

'Two blokes can't love each other like the way you're saying.' Lindsay looked so much older then and impossibly ugly. An imposter masquerading as Lindsay and doing a piss-poor job of it.

'We have.' Malcolm found courage in that knowledge.

He felt his strength return, at thinking of them together, not the lovemaking, although that too, but the times when they'd swam naked at desolate, pristine beaches and then lay together, entwined in the shade, with the bristly grass scratching at them and leaving marks long after they'd left. Reminding Malcolm of the moment, long after they'd left and the sunburn had healed. Or sometimes how he'd deliberately injure himself on a rock or a branch, to cause a cut or a bruise that would be a souvenir in place of a photograph.

Or the meals they'd shared together, hiding in plain sight in public. Lindsay would be having such a good time he'd forget himself and give Malcolm modicums of affection. A pinch on his cheek, a light slap across it, his hand scrunching at the jutting of his jaw and coming to rest briefly at the base of his chin, his hand passing across the small of his back like a bird skimming across the surface of a lake. Or mornings spent in Malcolm's bed in his squalid apartment in Darlinghurst. Him reading aloud to a mystified and mute Lindsay, who never looked more happy and handsome then when he was propped up and gilded by the morning sunlight poking through the ratty blinds.

Malcolm wanted that, all of that and everything else, even the bad stuff too, because the good vastly outweighed the bad.

'I know you think the secrecy is necessary, but I also know it makes you miserable.' Malcolm clasped his hands together, to prevent from letting them go rogue and try touching Lindsay, who sat primly stiff next to and far away from him, with an inscrutable expression, like his face forget what it was supposed to do.

'Marion needs to know,' Malcolm continued. 'No more of this godawful sneaking around.'

Another deep sigh, Lindsay blinked at him. 'Come on now.'

'Don't be like that.' Malcolm took a seat next to Lindsay and gazed outward, beyond the trees and the last vestiges of the daylight, to the cityscape just visible in the distance. So much industry, so much construction. So much promise that tomorrow would be better than today, bigger.

If they can build a skyscraper like that that can blot out the sun then Lindsay and he should be able to start a life together, Malcolm thought. 'Let's just go. Go to the ends of the Earth. Someplace with surf and sand and sun. Someplace remote. Ideally without many locals and with no mozzies. I know you're rich, I know you have more than enough money to leave to Marion to ensure she's comfortable for the rest of her life. Don't try telling me different.'

'I can't just abandon her for good. No explanation. No nothing. That's so cruel.'

'It is more cruel to keep going on with this lie though. Would it not be better to be yourself and be happy?' Malcolm's hand settled on Lindsay's knee, where it felt so right, like it was grooved and meant to sit there. Lindsay did not try shoving it off, or angling his leg away. Sometimes the tumult eased and Lindsay could be himself before he caught himself doing it.

'Me loving Marion is no lie,' Lindsay said.

'I'm not saying that, I know you love her and adore her and have such respect and admiration for her, much like I do with Isla. It's a sisterly love. So strong and pure that it's endured you a lifetime.'

'It has.' Lindsay regarded Malcolm's hand on his knee and his hand twitched on the bench twitched like it yearned to place itself atop it.

Malcolm took that as a good sign. 'But do you concede that it is different kind of love than you feel for me?'

Lindsay made to speak and couldn't.

Unable to restrain himself any longer, deciding that any walkers or any other park-goers could go to the Devil if they thought they could disrupt or alter the moment, Malcolm clasped both of Lindsay's hands in his. They were trembling but they came without resistance, so too Lindsay's eyes as Malcolm leant forward to kiss him, but Lindsay moved backward before their lips met. Malcolm's heart sank when he caught sight of Lindsay's eyes flitting around to ensure they were still alone.

'I love you and I know you love me in the same way,' Malcolm told Lindsay. 'That love has changed over time, to something so much more. I know that much, even though I can't adequately put it into words. I do know that virtually the whole world would not understand us, but I know that I don't need them to. All I need is you and that's all I need to be happy.'

And he meant every word and he allowed himself to believe that maybe the nights wouldn't seem so pitch-black and eternity-spanning with Lindsay next to him. Maybe his body warmth could keep that creeping chill of suicidal thoughts at bay.

'I do love you,' Lindsay haltingly said. 'But I'll never leave Marion. Or the life I have with her. I'm sorry, alright. I'm so sorry.' His hands were now the ones to hold Malcolm's and Malcolm felt himself breaking, with the understanding building inside him.

'If you don't tell her, I will.' He heard himself say to Lindsay.

Lindsay's face went to stone, as his eyes went ablaze. 'She wouldn't believe you.'

Malcolm took his hands back; they were still warm from Lindsay's, but that brought no warmth to his heart. 'I think she would.'

His new resolve must've shown, because Lindsay's face exploded with rampant fear, made him into a small, pathetic creature that dwelled in deep burrows. 'Would you really truly do that to me?'

'To make you see reason, I might.'

'By ruining my life?'

The self-pity pouring from him was fuelling the fires raging in Malcolm. 'I see it more as ending your old deceitful one and starting you on your new, happier one.'

'Well mate.' Lindsay leant forward toward him, his imposing build returned, his face coloured an unsightly crimson. 'Go try it and see what happens.'

Malcolm stayed still. 'I will then.'

Lindsay leapt up and began punching the bench, not a hair-breadth away from where Malcolm was sitting.

Malcolm tumbled off as the thick wooden slats reverberated from the barrage, crawled backward as fast as he could. Not that Lindsay was in pursuit, or so much as acknowledged he was even there.

There was a sharp crack sound and Malcolm hoped that that belonged to one of the slats on the bench and not a bone. The panting Lindsay lifted his hand and inspected it as if it had detached and was used by someone else before being returned to him. His knuckles were reddening and beaded with blood and his whole hand was starting to tremble, but the gaze he affixed on Malcolm was steady.

His eyes, his stance, all of it radiated menace and malice. This was a version of Lindsay that Malcolm had never witnessed before, instinctively cowered from.

Lindsay finally pointed a bloodied finger toward Malcolm. 'Stay away from me and my wife.'

'Lindsay,' Malcolm croaked, glad that he was already on the ground, doubtful that he could try rising, even if he put his all into it.

'You've been warned.' Lindsay set off then, his fedora askew.

Malcolm was too stunned to do much of anything save watch him go.

Lindsay crossed a few feet, before halting and rounding and returning and Malcolm's heart dropped as his hands half-raised as he was certain he was about to be transformed into a mound of gore.

But Lindsay ignored him, scanned the area for a moment, and then plucked up his pipe from where it tumbled in a bed of grass.

He then turned heel and stormed off with the sure footing of someone leaving something that offended them greatly by being in the same presence, sharing the same oxygen. Malcolm felt his eyes water and his chest heave, but he still managed to call out. 'I love you Lindsay Ward. I love you.'

But Lindsay didn't turn around or even slow his pace, and Malcolm wasn't even sure anymore if he had indeed called out to him, or if he had, if he were trapped in some sound vacuum, contained within one tiny pocket of Brett Park.

Either way, he wasn't brave enough to attempt to call out to Lindsay again. Malcolm only saw Lindsay's retreating form wipe at his face and wondered then if he was also battling as many tears as he himself was.

Winter

Kate Welsh

The flood stretched intrusively across the reserve, imposing itself over the pathways and surrounding the outdoor gym equipment.

Carol usually sought comfort from the routine of walking along the river bank each day, just her and Winter sniffing out the familiar territory. Today, though, the flood was ominous, filling Carol with a sense of angst. She let Winter off her lead. The white whippet pounded into the festering water, cavorting and kicking up spray behind her with glee.

Carol strode around the edge of the vast river cyst to the dirt track on the other side of the reserve. She loved observing the little wattle scrubs as they flowered at the first sign of Spring, but they were drowning now and well out of sight.

'Winter!' she called, trusting the dog would follow. She began to follow the alternate route that led away from the flood and towards a strip of grassland. After several seconds Carol realised the sounds of crazed sloshing had stopped. She turned. Despite her calling out repeatedly, Winter was nowhere in sight.

Carol walked back over to the edge of the flood, folded up her trousers and begrudgingly stepped in to go looking for Winter. Her feet were instantly swallowed by freezing water – the dog-walking runners did nothing to protect her. Within seconds her toes took on an aching throb that shot up her legs. She waded over to where she'd last seen the dog, yelling as she went, but still there was no sight of her.

'WINTER!' Carol wailed. She thought about having to go home without Winter, picturing her kids distressed and sobbing. Images swirled in her mind of Winter helplessly swept away in the raging river, getting lost, or perhaps running up to the road and being struck by a car. This was the last thing they needed, especially after everything that had happened.

The stress started to constrict Carol's throat. Her face throbbed with adrenalin and her stomach twisted in fear.

Suddenly a flash of white caught her eye through the trees at the other side of the flood. Carol churned through the water as fast as she could. As Carol got closer, the growling got louder. The dog had found a little patch of higher ground where the flood had receded a fraction at the edge of the bushland.

'Winter! COME!' she commanded, but the dog stayed put. 'Winter!' she scolded in the deepest voice she could muster.

The smell hit Carol before she realised what her dog had been eating. Winter stopped snarling and turned to face her pack-leader. With her head low and looking sheepish, she laid the rotting hand on the ground in apology.

Stunned, Carol froze. As suddenly as she had flipped into terror moments ago, she abruptly switched from it and stared at the hand. Then her breathing completely slowed. Another sense of terror began to throb through her as Carol's mind processed what was in front of her. Winter looked at Carol, waiting for some slight instruction about what to do with this thing, but Carol just watched, her icy toes forgotten.

At last – after what was an agonising wait for Winter – Carol finally gasped in air, took a step closer then crouched down, her eyes never leaving the hand. She examined it further, taking in its redness, its filthiness, its rawness. Having been saturated in the water, the flesh was puffy and peeling away, revealing a glimmer of bone.

Carol seemed unaffected by the out-of-date meat smell that was driving her dog insane. She brought a poo bag out from her coat. Without hesitation she picked the hand up by its middle finger, deposited it inside the black plastic bag and tied it up.

Standing, Carol placed it in her inside coat pocket. Urgency took over; there was something she needed to check.

'Come, Winter,' she said as she set off into the dense bush that surrounded the east side of the reserve. There wasn't a path, but she knew exactly where she was going.

Through the slick undergrowth she trod, moving damp wattle branches to the side and carefully stepping over rocks and decomposing wood. Tree ferns dripped leftover rain onto her as she disturbed them, and a leech attached itself to her left calf. Carol didn't notice.

As she made her way through the thick forest her mind was filled with other things. *Tom*. Picturing him walking in front of her, Carol remembered the last time they had come here and could sense his presence leering over her. As the memory flooded back, fear coursed through her. She had known he was about to do something dreadful to her, yet she had still followed him helplessly through the bush like a terrified animal.

After a half hour trek, Carol found herself again at the foot of the old hollow mountain ash. She looked up its mossy trunk to where the grey sky filtered through its branches. It was going to rain, just like last time. A little sob left her mouth.

'You know, this tree was planted by my great great-grandfather when they filled in the mine shaft,' Tom had said. 'If you look into the hollow, you'll see where it's caved in.'

Carol was shaking, trying to hold down the choking tears. This was where her life was going to end. 'I don't want to see,' she replied.

He grabbed her coat shoulder and pulled her towards the tree. Carol grasped hold of the hollow opening, hanging on for dear life. Tom yanked at her savagely, trying to rip her free. Carol looked up at Tom. His monster face was screwed up, so filled with rage and hatred for her. He was overpowering and too strong.

'Pllllleeeeaasse,' she cried.

She whispered the word again now as she approached the hollow. *'Please,'* she said. 'Please still be here.'

Carefully Carol inched further inside. The mouth of the mine was right in front of her. She reached for her phone and activated the torch mode. Kneeling down, Carol shone the light down the shaft.

At first, she wasn't sure what she could see. A year ago, she had thrown down as much soil as she could to cover him up. Carol strained her eyes and moved the light around. The shaft walls jutted downwards unevenly, and she couldn't make anything out.

Carol stretched herself face down on the ground and extended her head and upper body as far over the hole as she dared. Angling the light around again, she glimpsed a little patch of dark red approximately ten metres below. The colour stood out to her distinctly from its natural organic surroundings. It was a dirtier shade now, more earthy, but memories of Tom's red rain jacket flashed through her mind. He was still down there!

As relief filled Carol, she picked up on the smell, too. It was faint, but a distinct musty odour was rising up from the shaft. An image of the taxidermied animals at the museum came into her mind. Her fear of Tom's remains being swept out of the shaft because of the flooding subsided now that she knew he was still here. The flood waters obviously hadn't made it this far into the bush.

Carol had been about to give up, about to let go and give in to her violent ending. Suddenly a snapping Winter raced into the tree hollow, soaring up and ravaging Tom's face. He let go of Carol to push the dog away but stumbled backwards. A soul wrenching snap echoed out of the shaft as he fell.

A little whimpering behind Carol brought her back to the present, and she pulled away from the mine opening. Distress erupted as she reached out and sobbed into Winter's fur. The dog melded into her owner's arms and the two of them embraced each other, Winter comforting Carol. After several minutes Carol released the dog.

'Oh Winter, you good girl,' Carol said, fondling the dog's head. She then wiped the tears from her cheeks. 'Let's get out of here.'

Winter seemed to agree and led the way back out of the bush. Anxiety began to course through Carol again as she contemplated the hand. Could a fox have brought it up from the mine shaft? But then a chill shot up her spine – maybe it wasn't even Tom's? Was it decomposed enough to be his? With her lack of knowledge of rotting body parts, Carol thought back over a blur of crime documentaries. She concluded it was too fresh to be Tom's. She wondered if she should take it to the police. But surely, they would search the whole area and then maybe find Tom. She couldn't risk putting the kids through that; they were settled and not living in fear for the first time in their lives.

As she reached the carpark Carol opened her coat and retrieved the bag with its gruesome contents from her pocket. Her hands shaking, she put it into the dog poo bin. A shiver ran through her shoulders and she turned away.

'Good girl, Winter,' she said, unlocking the car to make their way back home. She hoped that this would be the last time Tom would come back to haunt her and Winter.

As Winter leapt into the boot, Carol took one last gaze around at the flood and the reserve. She felt at the mercy of the flood. What other secrets would it reveal as it receded over the coming days? She hoped there were no more random body parts anywhere nearby, praying that if there were, they had been swept elsewhere.

Perhaps she shouldn't come down here again in the future. The daily patrol of the area to remind herself that Tom really was dead and not coming back should maybe stop now.

She thought about those budding wattles she loved to see flower. She would miss them, but perhaps it was time for her to start her own springtime.

It had been a very long winter for Carol and her family.

It's Judgement Day, Bitch!

Beau Windon

I knew it would be an interesting day when I looked through the schedule of Judgements and saw Harley Finch on my list. Harley's was a peculiar case we debated for quite some time before a verdict was reached. Approaching my work bench, he smiled the smile of one who knew he was a good man, confident he'd get the Heaven he always dreamed of.

He greeted me with a respectful handshake. 'Nice to finally meet you, Saint Peter. Well, nice as can be given the circumstances.' His eyes flicked to the poster behind my bench. It featured a cat hanging from a branch with the phrase, 'Hang in there, baby!' written below. He rubbed the spot on his head where just days ago his brain had exploded out of.

'I'm sorry it took you so long to pass on. It looked immensely painful, but you fought so hard to stay. Most people would just hand over their wallet when a thug has a gun to their head.' I stopped to read his expression. He had a sadness in his eyes that could really ruin someone's day.

'I had something worth fighting for, a reason to keep my wallet and not give up my life.' He pulled out his wallet, opened it up and smiled. I snapped my fingers to create a chair for him. A second snap of my fingers created a cushion to comfort his bottom and a third snap brought forth a glass of water. I motioned that he take a seat.

'Oh, thank you. I didn't think this would take long enough to bother sitting,' he said, wriggling about to make himself comfortable. 'Can I ask you something?'

I considered him for a moment. I had a packed day of Judgements to get through, but I had allotted extra time for Harley due to the complications of his case. As he stared at me, all wide eyed and hopeful, I decided to let him ask his question and gave a nod.

'Are my wife and kids all right? I hope they're not too upset and that they'll get by without me.'

I smiled. 'You are a thoughtful man. Your wife

and kids are fine. The insurance payment is already being processed.'

'Oh, thank goodness.' He slumped back in his seat and mouthed a thank you to my chandelier, which I realised was meant to be aimed at the Heavens.

'You know he's right behind these gates. No need to thank a chandelier when the Heavens are here in front of you.'

He apologised and bowed his head in a sign of respect. 'So I can just make my way inside now then?' He stood up and reached out to shake my hand.

'Well, not so fast, Harley. Please sit.'

He sat down and put his hands in his lap. I wasn't sure if he was nervous or just impatient, but his legs were shaking like he needed to pee. 'I'm sorry, sir,' he said. 'I'm just excited to see my Ma and Pa. Ma passed away before I proposed to Jackie; I can't wait to tell her that she said yes and how beautiful she looked with Ma's old ring. And I gotta tell Pa that I finally left Dunder Mifflin and got a job with a more respectable company – he hated my old boss.'

'Well, let's get down to it then, shall we?' I gave him my best reassuring smile and opened *the* book.

'Harley Finch, by all accounts you've lived a good life. You've raised polite, confident children, been a faithful and loving husband, volunteered at a homeless shelter and fostered abandoned dogs in need of a home. You admirably fought for equal pay for the rest of your colleagues, even turning down a bribe. When you were only ten years old, you willingly got yourself beaten to a pulp sticking up for Scott Michael, even though you didn't like him. That bravery had a massive positive influence on Scott and he's gone on to do great things because of you. At fourteen, you dived into a lake to save an old lady from drowning. At twenty, you sat with a scared young girl all night while she waited for the first bus of the morning. You even attended church every Sunday of your life. You've been a good man. However ...'

'Oh no, what does 'however' mean? I've done everything possible to do the right thing. What's the 'however'? Why the 'however'?' He stood up and started pacing until I cleared my throat loudly and motioned him back to his chair.

'Come now, Harley, you had to have seen this coming.' We sat in silence. He stared at me as if I knew something that he didn't. 'Back when you were in primary school, you killed a boy.'

'Oh, that.' He smiled like he had just remembered the punchline to a joke. 'That was for a good reason. It was hardly unjustified.'

'And what, pray tell, is a good reason for murder?' I asked him, leaning forward.

'Well, he had a shiny Charizard card. Refused to trade it – wouldn't even listen to offers – yet every day he'd brag to everyone about his Charizard, first edition and shadowless. It was the crown jewel of the Pokémon card game. You can't brag about that card so much and not even entertain trade offers. That's evil.'

'And killing him wasn't?' I cocked my eyebrow.

'Well, no. It's a Charizard. *A fucking shiny Charizard!* You can't be a Pokémon Master without a Charizard. Everyone knows that, and he knew the risk that comes with owning one and being a smug dick about it. I offered him a shiny Blastoise and a shiny Zapdos for it and he just put his fingers in his ears and ran away.'

I nodded, taking in everything he was saying. The verdict had come down to me when we debated Harley's fate. I was the sole vote in determining his redemption or retribution. 'And so, would it have been fair if someone were to murder you for it? Poison you? Like you did that poor boy?'

He cackled like a mad man. 'No. Why would that be fair? I did the right thing. I listened to every single offer anyone made to me. No one ever made an offer good enough. This baby is my most valuable possession. I've carried it with me every single day of my life.' He opened his wallet and pulled out – what was still – a shiny Charizard card in mint condition, protected in a clear plastic sleeve. 'It's proof that I'm the very best ... like no one ever was.'

'I see. Yet it is still murder, and murder is a crime worthy of hell.' I picked up my hell stamp and looked him over. The fearful expressions were always the hardest thing about this job. I gave a nod to the cloud carpet next to his chair and a small fiery hole opened up.

'But I've been a good man. Just last week I nursed an injured bird back to health. I was about to run a marathon to raise money for cancer research. I've repented for my sin, if you can even call it a sin.' He stood up, tears welling in his eyes. 'It's a fucking Charizard. *A Charizard!* You don't have any idea how important that is. This card has made my life worth living.'

I put my hell stamp down and walked around the table to him, opening my arms and taking him in a warm embrace. 'I'll tell you what; I'll make you an offer.'

'You want me to suck ...' he choked off the end of his thought, held back his tears and dropped to his knees.

'*What!* Jesus. No. That's –' I flicked him on the nose. 'No.' He stopped crying and looked up at me. 'I don't do that. I'll let you into Heaven, on one condition. You give me your Charizard.'

'What?' he stuttered.

'I'll give you a pass, let you into the pearly gates, in exchange for your Charizard. You said you're open to all offers. Well, this is the most important offer of your existence.' I walked over to the gates and unlocked them, holding it open just long enough for him to hear Elvis playing his daily concert. 'Well?'

He stared at his Charizard long and hard. 'Could you maybe throw in a couple of shiny Pokémon cards to sweeten the deal?'

'No can do, Harley. Heaven is the most I can offer you.'

A tear ran down his cheek as Harley kissed the card and placed it in my hand.

'No trade backs,' I said, patting his shoulder and waving him through the gates. He walked in like a man conflicted and fearful of buyer's remorse. Once he was gone I pulled out my phone and called Jesus.

'Guess who has a shiny Charizard, bitch!'

Life Happens When

Erin McWhinney

You can hear it before you see it. The shifting south-westerly that carries the winter rain up from the strait. It sounds different, this wind, as it moves through the trees. Thinner, icier. It signals a change.

This wind assaults rather than caresses the gum leaves. It does the same to your face when you leave the house, phone in one pocket and keys in the other. Then the drizzle starts and you wish you'd grabbed an umbrella as well.

You can feel it before you see it. The shift in mood, the subtle rise in electrical tension, his back arching like a bristling cat. You try to play nice, placate, but he's gone. It's better not to try. Just leave.

But you do try, despite the knowing. Try to coexist. Speak only in quiet music and move like water. Look up at him from under the rippling surface.

You can hear it before you see it. The faint whir of bicycle tyres in the wet. But you've already stepped out blindly into the street and it's too late to take that step back. The collision is more of a brush, a clumsy side-swipe with a flash of blue and a caustic bark – *Watch it, cunt!* – but it's the loss of balance, the tumble backwards onto the curb that gets you.

What did he say before you left? He said something, spat it rather, from his place on the couch but you were halfway out the door. Time only allowed you to grab phone and keys, but you'll be back.

What were the words? Those words you want to wield like weapons. Maybe it's best you didn't hear. You'll be back when the wind turns, when the Antarctic bite has melted and forgiven you.

You can hear it, feel it, smell it before you see it. The music of an ECG monitor, of quiet words in surround sound, of squeaking trolley wheels and rubber soles, all beneath a patina of ear-ringing. The dry-mouth sensation and sandpaper tongue, throbbing head, hard bed. The disinfectant.

Watch it, cunt! You couldn't remember the words before but you can now, in the fever-dream wilds of anaesthesia. Your blood feels hot and is coursing through you like fire. Your heart is running marathons while the rest of your body is a collection of lead weights that now serve to drag you to the bottom of the ocean like cinder blocks chained to a mafia traitor. He spat the words as you went out the door with only your phone and keys. Does it not seem strange to you that he was wearing a blue bike helmet while sitting on the couch?

You can feel it before you see it. The hand on yours. A heavy, obstinate hand that rests wearily on the IV needle taped to your skin. You try to open your eyes, to speak, but everything is glued shut. The hand is on your head now, clammy, and a far-off voice says

'Shhh, you're okay now.' The voice is familiar, but not a comfort.

***

When you are finally able to open your eyes, you tell him you're going for a walk. He asks how you can go out when you have a concussion. Outside the wind is blowing gently from the north and the sun is tinting gum leaves golden. You can't imagine staying inside, and you suspect that maybe you don't have a concussion after all. You don't remember how you could have sustained such an injury. But your body instinctively knows that his mood will turn, inevitably, if you stay.

Short Story Competition

Short story writing is a form of writing that holds all sorts of possibilities. While it might seem restrictive due to the length, anything is possible – from a traditional story with a typical arc, to a snapshot in time, to something more exploratory.

Anybody interested in short story writing should read the work of great short story authors like Ryan O'Neil, Laura Elvery, A.S. Patric, Julie Koh, and Laurie Steed, among others.

There are two difficulties in judging:
1. these stories are unedited. So, sometimes, you see the potential in something that isn't quite fully realised, and might've done with another revision, or feedback from other readers.
2. it's all subjective. Give the same group of stories to another reader, and they'd likely place them differently.

Marissa's Present – Highly Commended
Dominique Davidson
The verisimilitude in 'Marissa's Present' is eerie. The author has either researched exhaustively, or has genuine experience working in a mortuary. There's a nice dark tone that builds the story piecemeal.

If you are but a dream – 3rd Place
James Karantonis
This story asks a simple question: *what do dreams mean to us?* There are a lot of great themes and ideas here. I think it could even be explored as a novel, or novella.

This story felt like a hybrid between Phillip Dick and Isaac Asimov.

Vetiver – 2nd Place
Zachary Pryor
A haunting story about dealing with loss, facing the past, coming home, and trying to find our place in the world. There is a melancholy to the voice that makes you feel the protagonist's lament.

Fever – 1st Place
Rebecca Howden
A nice tone that playfully explores our desire for notoriety and gratification, and to what costs we'll pursue that. The voice is strong throughout, and the story effortlessly alternates between the various plot threads, intertwining them and coming to … well, you'll have to read it.

For anybody who didn't get through, don't be discouraged. Writing's about perseverance.

My good friend Laurie Steed once said to me that every rejection brings your story one submission closer to its eventual home.

Les Zig, Competition Judge

Fever

Rebecca Howden

Yoga isn't just *stretching*. The magic happens when you still your mind long enough to actually feel the pain that courses through you like stormwater, then breathe through it anyway.

From the start, when Bliss would say things like that, Ashley would roll her eyes and harpoon her elbow into my ribs. And at first I'd smirk and I'd listen to her sarcastic whispers. It was always me and Ashley then; me playing the role of sidekick, her slightly dishevelled understudy.

But quietly, I was captivated by Bliss. Maybe it was her fame or her sweetly overcrowded smile, or the way she'd say 'You're the best' when I brought her a matcha latte. Already, she was under my skin, flowering in my bloodstream. And I would do anything she said.

Before Bliss, it was a long, cobwebbed winter. Something inside me was unspooling. The days were funereal, all wet streets strewn with leaves, cold hair whipping around faces. There were spores of loneliness in the air around me.

Still, I faked it. Look at me, rubbing rosehip oil into thirsty skin, into the crinkling ends of my hair. I brightened myself with shimmery bronzer and peach lipgloss. I made sunny Instagram posts – a green smoothie bowl from a Sunday months ago, pomegranate seeds shining like jewels. (*'Post-workout breakfast! So invigorated after an early morning run on the beach.'*) I sat cross-legged on the floor for my morning meditation and tried my best to hush the wild, thrashing hurricane in my head.

You need a really strong affirmation for that, though.

At the studio, I'd teach my yoga classes. Girls wrapped in different coloured workout tights flowed through vinyasas; a rippling stream of black and neon and ocelot print. There were breaks in the kitchen with Ashley and the others, sipping peppermint tea and crunching on goji nut bars.

The girls had all quit caffeine so I pretended I had too, jolting myself alive with double espressos in secret afterwards. Ashley would talk about her intermittent fasting diet and the new booty blast program she was creating and what some other influencer had posted on Instagram. I'd study my chipped manicure, longing for something. For time to pass, for anything.

The days were anonymous, soaked with something like despair. Until Bliss swept in, a burst of mermaid hair and coconut-scented skin, and it was like a window opening, letting in cold, bright daylight.

She was a bit of a celebrity in our world. Bliss Crowhurst, swiftly becoming the wellness goddess *du jour*, complete with a brand-new bestselling cookbook and a dizzying YouTube following. She had freckles across her nose and marketing in her bloodstream, and she had the star power to take the studio to the next level.

We all knew her story; the series of disasters she'd overcome. First, a mysterious, chronic fatigue-type illness, which she healed with nutrition and mindful fitness. Then her best friend died in a surfing accident (or a suicide – that was unclear; Bliss was now a passionate advocate for both beach safety and mental health, and also, vaguely, friendship.) In her grief, she escaped to a yoga retreat in the Sri Lankan beach town of Mirissa. She spent salt-spritzed weeks meditating, perfecting her dragonfly pose and vlogging her personal healing journey against the hush of the Indian Ocean. One day, she decided to take the train up to Colombo for an overnight trip. The next morning she got up early to stroll the colourful streets and the seafront promenade. That was Easter Sunday – the day six bombs blasted through churches and luxury hotels across the city.

It was the best thing that could have happened for her personal brand.

In the days and weeks after Colombo, her videos went viral – tears down her cheeks, her voice gorgeously husky as she described the horror she'd witnessed. She launched an online fundraiser for the bombing victims, promising 50% of the profits from her six-week mind-body transformation guide. Blog articles, podcast interviews and a book deal quickly followed. And just like that, we all knew the name Bliss Crowhurst.

Now the studio blossomed with peach-coloured lilies. Her suggestions became gospel; the space was brushed with her feather-light touches. We got expensive new yoga mats and a coral feature wall. Essential oil diffusers beamed out an island scent of sweet vanilla and caramel. The front desk was stacked with copies of her book – a collection of colourful salads and raw treats, adorned with her musings on resilience – and jars of the organic granola blend she'd collaborated with a local brand to put her name on.

She was ridiculous, obviously. And yet. She was so vigorously alive, pulsing with an energy I wanted to feel. From that first day, I was drinking up her movements. I found myself moving as if she was watching; sauntering like her, head tall and arms loose. Trying to soak up some of her liquid grace.

Only Ashley refused to be bewitched by her. 'I found out her real name,' she told me one afternoon. 'It's *Genevieve*.'

We were alone in the sun-drenched upstairs studio space. Ashley had one leg stretched high up the wall. She was used to being the star around here – the iridescent Ashley Zhang, with her strong legs and impish smile and genius for designing yoga-HIIT fusion workouts. She was the name that lured in adoring flocks of girls, made them all too happy to hand over their membership fees. She was the one whose abs were #goals.

I bent over in ragdoll pose, my plait reaching towards the floor in a long, wheat-coloured rope.

'I just don't think she's *genuine*,' Ashley said.

I didn't say anything. We kept stretching.

There we were, all the lead studio girls. Me and Ashley, and Priyanka and Tiff and Katja and Beth and Mei. All of us svelte and straight-backed, variations on a theme. We sat in a softly breathing crescent, Bliss in front of us on the studio stage. She smiled, coral lipgloss bright.

'You're all in a unique and powerful position here,' she said, looking at each of us slowly. 'You received a calling to guide people on their wellness journey. But to transform lives, you need to make sure you're showing up as fully and authentically as you can. You need to step into your power.'

I swear, that's how she talked. Like it was an Instagram caption, like she was born in test-tube labelled 'manifestation goddess'. And yet, I couldn't take my eyes off her – her long collarbone, the dip in her throat, where a tiny silver star pendant was nestled. Somehow, I could feel the brittle edges of myself dissolving.

'You all know my story,' she said. 'Everything I've been through. And the truth is, in my darkest times, I let myself become a victim. That was the worst thing that happened to me – not all the trauma I experienced. As soon as I stepped out of that, I found so much alignment and I discovered my real inner strength.

'But I see some of you still hiding in that victim mentality. You're too scared to let your light shine. You're too scared to *do the work*, and do what it takes to get what you want.'

And she looked directly at me. Her eyes were the slippery grey of dolphin skin.

'So,' she said. 'What are you going to do about it?'

Falling in love is a fever. Summer was coming, the days swelling up. I wanted to be around Bliss, to understand her shifts in mood; how she'd go from quiet and steely to surging with rosy-cheeked warmth. I wanted to earn that dazzling smile, to catch a glimpse of that one slightly-crooked eyetooth, like a little fang saying hello.

Her big idea for the studio was to launch a retreat offering – luxury escapes down the coast, with a revitalising schedule of yoga, mindfulness and fitness. So I offered to help her, and it became the focus of my weeks. 'Oh my god, you're the best,' she'd say, when I showed her a sample menu or a cool hike I'd found. 'Damn, we make a good team.' And just like that – suddenly, miraculously – I felt chosen.

At lunchtimes with the sun blazing we'd buy pressed juices and power walk around the park, and she'd get me talking about things usually left in dark boxes in my mind. The ex-boyfriend who loved Fleetwood Mac, which meant only Lucy the bartender, who also loved Fleetwood Mac, could really understand him. The ambitions I'd once had to write, until I realised I had nothing to say. The way Ashley would sometimes forget to invite me places.

'Ashley doesn't want you to reach your potential,' Bliss said. 'She wants you to stay small and be her follower. That's the role you play for her.'

Those afternoons now are a kaleidoscope in my mind. Our bright white Nikes, the leafy sky. Bliss biting into a wet green apple, the crunch of her teeth sinking in. I watched her chew and I could almost taste the tangy juice. That burst of flavour, painfully sweet.

Ashley was always smouldering, dark eyes narrowed. 'Did you hear the way she was talking, as if she *owns* the place?' she hissed, grabbing my arm after a staff meeting.

She kept finding threads to tug at. 'That story she told about her childhood dog dying? I listened to this podcast interview she did for Mamamia where she said she's never *had* a pet.' She'd find slivers of insults in Bliss's words and fume over them for weeks. 'She told me my sweet potato salad looked carb-y.' 'She said I was *brave* to wear white leggings.'

And I let her talk. But the more I surrendered to the magnet pull of Bliss, the more Ashley's voice became a seashell sound.

The temperature kept rising, the hot breath of summer on our necks. In between teaching classes and planning Bliss's retreats and actually creating social media content again, my days were a whirl of adrenaline and sweaty skin. Sometimes I'd notice a quiet fury brewing between Ashley and Bliss – sharp glances, hushed conversations, faces grim – but I didn't care. I was focused, productive again.

Yoga was still the one thing that could always soothe me – that moment when you feel the rhythms of your body and breath sync up; the bursting feeling of rising up from a sun salutation. I liked to flow through simple sequences and teach a beginner-friendly class, but Bliss said I wasn't pushing myself hard enough. I needed to master the more advanced poses, she said. And so she helped me, guiding me through my scorpion-leg handstand. 'It's all in your mindset,' she kept saying, her hands adjusting my form, her minty breath close. 'Focus on your core. Don't overthink it.'

So I practiced and practiced. And eventually, I got it. I held the pose, my back curved, my legs strong in the air. And for a second, I felt really alive. I was vigorous and bright, just like Bliss.

I was filling up my glass drink bottle at the water fountain, Ashley slinking around me like a cat. Her inky black ponytail poured down her back.

'So, I was asking Bliss about her fundraiser for Sri Lanka,' she said. 'Like, how she organised it, who she actually gave the money to. 'Cause I couldn't remember what specific charity it was for.'

'I think it was for the Red Cross,' I said. I added a drop of peppermint oil to my water, took a sip. I felt cool and open in my chest. 'Or maybe like a local relief charity there.'

'But I don't know,' Ashley said, twisting the end of her hair in her fingers. 'She was so weird about it. Like she just got angry and wouldn't answer any of my questions.'

'Maybe because it seemed like you were accusing her of something.'

'Well,' she said archly.

Suddenly I felt overheated. The room seemed to tilt a little; my blood sugar low after my workout. I rolled my eyes. Ashley and her constant drama. The girl just could not handle being second best.

'Anyway, it's not just that,' Ashley said. 'I've been talking to some people on Instagram. Looking through her old posts and stuff. There's all kinds of things that don't add up.'

'Ash,' I said. 'Just stop.'

I spent Christmas back home in Perth with my family, waiting for a text from Bliss. The heat was simmering; the days stretched out endlessly. I went running on the beach with my brother. I read the first ten pages of *Daring Greatly*. I deleted Instagram from my phone, and reinstalled it a day later.

I waited to hear from her, and I never did.

After New Year's, the studio stayed closed for another week. It was the perfect chance for us to try out the retreat concept Bliss and I had been planning; double it as a team planning retreat for the year ahead. So we packed our resistance bands and essential oils and neon bikinis and we all went down to the coast together, me and Bliss and all the girls. Even Ashley, because we all knew the studio was nothing without Ashley Zhang.

The coastline curved like a wineglass; turquoise water blinked in the sun. This trip was a chance to revitalise, Bliss said, but we were also there to challenge ourselves and work hard. Each morning we'd wake early for sunrise yoga and guided meditation by the pool, before a nourishing breakfast of organic granola and coconut yoghurt and summer fruit. The rest of the day would be filled with mindset and resilience workshops, team goal setting sessions, active excursions, and more yoga and fitness challenges.

It quickly became clear Bliss would be running the show. My role in putting this all together, all the hours and sweat and spreadsheets, faded into the background, and Bliss took her natural place at the front of the pack. It was fine, I told myself. I didn't mind. But I couldn't explain that quiet ache, a dull stone pitted deep below my ribcage.

At night, I fell asleep early in a twin bed next to Ashley's, all my muscle fibres throbbing. Above me, a familiar fog of loneliness was hovering, darkly.

A morning swim, the water deliciously cool. I was alone; the others had all gone on a walk into town. In the quiet, the pool water was rippling and blue. Then Ashley burst from the house, calling my name.

'I need to talk to you,' she said, breathlessly. Her eyes were dark and wide, like a nocturnal animal, glinting strangely. And so I pulled myself up to the edge of the pool. Ashley sat down next to me, slipping her tanned feet into the water. Our toenails were painted the same shade of coral.

'So,' she said. 'I've been investigating some more, about Bliss. No – just listen for a sec.'

She grabbed my arm with her small, cool hand, held onto it loosely below the elbow.

'I found this guy Josh, who was at that retreat in Sri Lanka with her. Like, a typical meditation bro. And we were chatting about everything, and all the weird things about Bliss. And *he said* on the day of the bombings he saw her at a bar in Mirissa. Like, nowhere near Colombo.'

I felt a pulse inside me.

'She wasn't *there* when it happened,' she said.

'Maybe he just saw someone who looked like her,' I said. 'Or he's thinking of a different day.'

'No, he's positive. He was like obsessed with her. He said she went to Colombo a couple of weeks before that, but she was definitely back in Mirissa at Easter. When he saw her posting about it he thought it was weird, but he wasn't going to get involved and say anything.'

She let go of my arm and pulled out her phone. I blinked at the screen as she scrolled. The bubbles of their conversation shimmied in front of me. It was so hot; the sun was already burning viciously.

'That doesn't mean anything,' I said.

'Are you serious? It means she lied about witnessing a terrorist attack just to get attention. And then she had that fundraiser that I don't think was even real. This is *insane*.'

'You don't know that,' I said. I wiped at my forehead. The heat was making me dizzy. 'You don't know anything about her.'

Ashley just looked at me, a hard, black gleam in her eyes.

'Neither do you,' she said.

That night, Ashley didn't come to dinner. She was sick, Mei told us, all feverish and vomiting. Typical

Ashley melodrama. We switched up our sleeping arrangements so she'd have a room to herself. She stayed in there the whole next day too, and the next.

Now it was four days into the trip, and I'd still barely had a second to talk to Bliss. She was busy playing camp leader, always surrounded. I'd put Ashley's theories away in the attic of my mind. They were just rumours; I didn't care. I wanted to be chosen by Bliss again.

That afternoon, we hiked along a rocky coastal trail. In towns not too far from here, furious bushfires were swallowing homes and land and wildlife, and a sooty scent lingered in the air, making sure we didn't forget. I thought maybe I could talk to Bliss then, but Priyanka and Katja had her ensnared in a deep conversation about intermittent fasting a few paces ahead of me. I kept my eyes focused on my hiking boots, the rhythmic crunch of each step, steady as a heartbeat. I wondered if they'd see it, if they looked back at me; the neediness seeping from my pores.

At a shimmering cove, we slithered out of our shorts and tank tops, let our ponytails and fishtail braids loose. For a moment, I closed my eyes behind my Ray-Bans. I stood still and listened to the silver hush of waves, the hiss of kombucha bottles being opened, peals of girl laughter – the effervescent sounds of summer. When I opened my eyes, Bliss and Priyanka were down by the water, posing for photos Tiff was taking on her phone. Their bodies were curved in dancer pose – one arm reaching out in front, one leg extended out behind, foot nestled in hand. They were beautiful.

I lay back on my elbows in the hot sand. A darkness was opening up inside me, wistfulness coursing through my body. Wistfulness, or quietly growing despair.

Back at the villa, I took a long, cool shower. I tried to practise mindfulness, force my attention on the pelting water rhythm instead of the dull panic rising from my belly. This is water, I said to myself. This is water, this is water, this is water. I dried off and threw on a white cotton dress. Now, I thought. Now I'll find Bliss and we can really talk, and this shuddering in my chest will stop.

She was out by the front gate with Priyanka. Priyanka, with her big dark eyes like a lemur and her impossible flexibility, leaning against the bluestone wall. Her neon yellow bikini was blinding.

'Oh hey, babe,' Bliss said. 'Pri and I are just heading into town for a sec.'

And I waited for them to invite me along. I waited and they didn't say anything.

'Oh, okay,' I said. 'Have fun.'

'We'll catch up later, okay?' Bliss said, touching my wrist lightly. And the look of pity in her eyes – well. It hit me right in the ribcage, hard.

I watched them walk away, their brown backs and salt-scrunched hair. Then Bliss stopped and looked back over her shoulder.

'Oh yeah,' she said, giving me her brilliant, crooked-toothed smile. 'Can you check on the caterers for tonight for me?'

I stood still as they continued down the path. The sound of their laughing voices swam through the thick air. I heard Bliss say, 'You're the best, Pri.'

❦

That night there was a party out by the pool. I lay upstairs on my bed, my temples throbbing. Out the window, I could see constellations of fairy lights strung up around the yard, the pool water alien blue in the dark. Indie pop music simpered through the air, trembling through the walls to my bones. I felt an overwhelming sense of nothingness. I didn't want to be here.

I looked over at my suitcase, a jungle of colourful activewear spilling out of it. And for a second I thought – I could leave. I imagined getting on a bus, watching the beach roll away in the inky darkness, my own face ghostly in the window. I knew I'd never do it, but for a few minutes I indulged the fantasy, played at packing up my things. I gathered my sports bras, my running shorts, and pressed them into my bulging bag. To be the one walking away from Bliss, from Ashley, from the juice cleanses, from all of it – the idea was surreally glorious.

My hand caught something tucked into the inside pocket of my suitcase. I pulled it out. Two small plastic bottles, travel containers for beauty products. But they weren't mine. I held them up to the light. They were both empty except for a few drops of liquid. Strange. I closed the suitcase and lay back on the bed.

My mind went to Ashley. She'd be in her room now too, still sick or faking it. I thought of all those nights last summer in her backyard – a Christmas tree scent, my ribs aching with laughter. Then two days ago, Ashley telling me those crazy things about Bliss, her eyes sizzling. The strange nausea inside me swelled. The girl was jealous and overdramatic, but she was shrewd. And I had to admit, I'd seen her detective skills before.

I sat up, knotted my hair on top of my head, slipped into my Birkenstocks. I didn't belong to

Bliss. I didn't belong to Ashley either. But I had to at least hear what else she thought she knew.

My breath caught in Ashley's doorway.

Ashley was crumpled up in bed, sweaty and pale. Bliss was sitting in a floral chair next to her, holding out a glass of green juice. Ashley was drinking slowly through a pink straw, her hands quivering. She barely looked conscious.

A sound came from my throat and Bliss looked up at me. A tiny flash of something – panic, fury – startled her features. Then she dissolved into a smile.

'Just checking on the patient,' she said softly. 'Make sure she gets her antioxidants.'

She reached out to smooth Ashley's hair.

'Olive leaf extract,' she said. 'Tastes like shit, but it heals everything.'

She turned back to me, smiling, but her eyes were still.

'What are you doing? Go join the party,' she said.

Ashley pushed the glass away and slumped back, curled onto her side. I'd never seen her so wilted and small.

'Ash?' I said. Her face was the colour of cement,

covered in a wet slick. She moaned a little, mumbled something. I touched her forehead. It was burning. A rush of pins and needles went through me.

'Bliss, I really don't think she's okay,' I said.

'She's fine,' Bliss soothed. 'Go on, you should go outside.'

And then Ashley started convulsing.

'*Ash*,' I yelled. I tried to hold her by the shoulders, to still her violent shaking. Her body was rigid. Her breath came out in hoarse, desperate gasps. I looked around frantically; I didn't have my phone.

'*Bliss*. Call someone. Fuck, what do we do?'

But Bliss didn't move. I scrambled at the bedside table. Ashley's phone must be there; the girl always had her phone. The lamp and the green smoothie glass fell in an angry crash. A dizzying blackness was swimming around the corners of my vision.

'Calm down,' Bliss said quietly.

And I looked at her, her serene face and long, crossed legs. I looked at the broken glass winking from the floor, the dregs of green smoothie in a sludgy pool. A flash in my mind – the unfamiliar travel bottles in my suitcase. And suddenly I knew.

'Bliss,' I said. 'Seriously, we have to get help. *Now*.'

And she smiled, her grey eyes smoky and cool.

'Do we?' she said.

Vetiver

Zachary Pryor

I hadn't planned on returning home, but Mum got sick. Technically speaking she'd been sick for a while but refused to tell anyone. It wasn't like, whoops there goes my health, she'd been declining for months. Now she's in hospital, supine, blue tubes sticking in and out of her. Arduously breathing. She's going to die.

It's a cold Friday. Dad picks me up from the airport. The clouds are swirls of ice cream on the horizon.

Good to see you champ, Dad shakes my hand as I emerge through the terminal gate. I guess we've become that family who refer to each other by previously unused nicknames. Maybe I should respond with a surfing chukka.

As if I'm some sort of deity who can control the movements of the sky, he tells me: You've brought in the rough weather. We were hoping for some of that Bondi sun mate.

He takes my worn gym bag and we head to the car.

I could have been one of those people who did research on Mum's condition. But the idea of learning about what was festering round her body broke a tiny bit of my heart. I grew numb. If had a brother or sister, they might have done the sleuthing. Dad wouldn't lift a finger.

It's difficult to talk about with my friends, so I don't. When we're in bars, expanding our waistlines with $12 parmas and Marrickville craft beer and talking about our families, I stay silent. I'm loud when it's about work, who we fuck, what we read, what we watch on Netflix.

Like a banana left out in the sun, Mum had deteriorated fast and I couldn't keep it to myself anymore. I told a couple of them and returned to Melbourne for a few days.

Dad pulls up to the broken bitumen, the pockets of unruly shrubs and the zebra stripes of flaking white and tired weatherboard.

Things are a bit of a mess, he apologises. I nod and follow him inside. He isn't kidding. With Mum indisposed, the house has become a bachelor pad: crusted baked beans on plates, knives still smeared with vegemite next to the sink, pot plants limp and browning.

I head to my room.

The only thing that's changed in eight years is the bedspread—yellow flowers instead of nautical stripes. I collapse onto them. It's dark outside when I wake. I drag my feet down the hall, toward the broken noise of the television. Dad's already a few tins deep.

Get your coat, we'll go see her, he says.

Footscray Hospital smells of chlorine. Stark lights. Friendly people smile and type away. Everyone is on a mission.

We're here to see Ruth Anderson. I know she's on the second floor, Dad says to one of the receptionists.

I follow Dad. His tufts of hair have greyed since I last saw him and his elbow is sticking through a hole in his coat. I don't mention that I gave him some money several months ago to keep the lights on and enough for a new coat, even if it's just from the

Salvos. I disinfect my hands with the cold, lemony sanitiser. Be brave, I remember Jean telling me. My best friend's done this before, the awkward end-of-life dance with her father only several months prior.

Surprisingly, Mum looks much as she did eight years ago, though the textured wrinkles of her face are now smooth as playdough. She lies there breathing softly, a lilac blanket around her shoulders. I take a seat and watch her. Dad paces.

I've been here for weeks, back and forth, he says. From where? He doesn't have a job to go back and forth from. He must mean the house. "The Shack" I announced to a friend once upon a time.

I take her hand, steady my own breathing, blink back a few tears. And we watch. A hospital is hardly the place to find transcendence, though the wavy green lines on her heart monitor have a soporific effect the longer I watch.

A few hours tick by. Dad punctuates the conversation, trying to remember the 'good times', which I can count on both hands. He finally falls asleep and drool gathers on his collar. I get up, put on my jacket and leave the hospital. Visiting hours are over.

Standing in the park outside, bathing in golden halogen lamplight I flick through my phone, looking at apps. I've adjusted my status to: Visiting. Yellow boxes of different men tightly packaged like tetras appear on the screen. Many of them in various stages of undress.

I don't want to go home. Not tonight.

Standing in the park, toes numb, I message someone whose tiny little square features a cowlick and dimples:

Hey

Hey

Up to? Keen?

Drink? I'm not in the area but I can be in about twenty mins

Modern day romance is punctuated by fewer and fewer characters. After several back and forth messages I find myself in an Uber, heading across town to meet him.

The bar he's chosen is dripping with speakeasy sensibility. Dimmed globes and mocha bentwood chairs. London Grammar flowing from the speakers. I smile as I walk through, seeking out the dimples. He's sitting there in a black shirt, a glass of plum red wine in a giant tumbler. He smiles as I approach, I notice a small gap between his teeth.

Good night? He says.

Average, at best. I reply, taking a seat. He motions to the waiter, who takes my order.

You're visiting, where from?

I flew in from Sydney this morning. My mother's in hospital, just a short trip to make sure she's okay, I lie.

That sucks man, I'm sorry. How long you been living interstate?

I moved there the summer after school and never left. You like Sydney? I ask. It's the inevitable question. The great rivalry.

It'll never beat Melbourne, but I don't mind it. I travel there for work all the time.

He continues to talk, and I drink. He orders another round. He tells me he's a consultant. Something fancy involving Artificial Intelligence and robots that chat to customers online. I'm perplexed but intrigued. He touches my hand and goose bumps ripple up my arm.

My place is just around the corner, he grins, audacious.

I'm keen, I nod.

Once we're back at his place, he takes off all my clothes, I take off his. His mouth tastes like wine. He lays me on my stomach with my head pressed gently into the pillow. He kisses my neck and holds my hips. He makes my body feel like hot oil.

Afterwards he hugs me, one arm over mine and breathes against my ear. It feels nice to be held. To be still. He drifts off and lets me go, rolling onto the other side of the bed. The sheets feel silky on my skin. As I lie awake, thinking about Mum, I wonder if she even knew I was in the room.

I wake and exhale silver ghosts. As I gain consciousness, I remember this is not my bedroom. The oatmeal sheets are soft to touch. The throw: chic and threadbare. Something purchased from Country Road, pretty but impractical. The thick, veiny leaves of a fiddle leaf—it's alive, I could never.

Morning, he says and reaches down to kiss my forehead. Minty breath. Standing over me, changing into a charcoal wool suit. I smile.

Outside, a thin rim of frost gathers on the window. He sprays a cologne and particles of vetiver fill the room. The fragrance looks luxe in its indigo, glass triangle bottle. I get to my feet and move around the room to collect my things. I'm picking up pieces off a puzzle: shoes, once white; ripped jeans, purchased torn. What was it they said about imposter syndrome?

He strokes my arm and says: I'm heading to work. Can you make it home okay? I'll message you.

Within seconds, his briefcase is in his hand and he's out the door. I squeeze into my jeans, hold my shoes in one hand and step out into the hall. Blackbutt floorboards cool on the balls of my feet. I look to the front door. My reflection distorts in the green and red glass pressed together with lead. I stroll back down the hallway, into the interior, treasures await.

This is a man who collects modern art. Above a console I see canvases covered in splashes of black and white and red, framed in blond wood. Beneath are family photos in twisty, silver frames. Loving parents holding their son in a tight embrace. There are many large, glossy appliances in the kitchen. I finger the coffee machine, leaving oily marks. Pulling out a pod from the jar next to it I help myself to a cup.

The coffee is strong, and the marble bench is cold against my lower back. Looking around it's clear this is a man who enjoys high ceilings, uncomfortable timber benches instead of dining chairs, light grey couches and soft-hued throw cushions.

I am not one of those people.

I wash out the mug and retreat, pop on my shoes on and leave.

The house stands apart from the others attached to it, like a red brick of Lego in a pile of white. Across the road stands a new apartment complex –

boxed windows behind pokey balconies like a large silver spaceship. The banksia trees on the pavement writhe within their little cages.

I walk to the main strip. The clanging of the level crossing halts the traffic for the oncoming train. The peeling blue station sign reads *Ripponlea*. I think of a ribbon, floating in the wind, twisting into the trees or the powerlines. I think of my friend Leigh, sandy haired, beach obsessed. The handsomeness of the place reveals itself through squashed Victorian brick homes with ornate fences, trees that have dropped all their leaves, groomed lapdogs prancing. In my daze I almost miss the train but jump on just as the doors rudely beep me inside. I sit next to the window and I read the news on my phone to pass the time.

I get home and shower. The hot water scalds my skin pink and washes away any lingering vetiver smell. Towelling myself dry, my arms are irritated by the rough texture. His towels wouldn't be like this—probably purchased in a plush set, they'd be discarded once showing signs of age.

I check my phone for the time. It's almost visiting hours in the hospital. I put on jeans and a fresh tee.

I'm ready to see Mum, I call out to Dad as I walk through the house.

He's sitting at the table, sorting through a worn cardboard box and not attending to the trashed kitchen.

Here you go champ, Dad says and hands me an emerald green book.

It's a photo album. Abruptly empty halfway through, ending with a photo of me in a plastic rain jacket about three years old standing in a puddle of water. Mum and Dad, excited by the prospect of having a child eagerly documented everything: first steps, first Easter egg, first time at the beach. Then life got in the way and the new child stopped being special. The bright spark of a shiny toy soiled by the routine of parenting.

Something for you to remember her by. When the time comes, Dad shrugs and looks away.

It's a nice gesture. We're not the kind of family that hug, so we stand there in silence until Dad gets the right idea to fetch his keys and we can get to the hospital.

Catching up with friends last night? he asks while we're driving.

Something like that, yeah.

I stare out the window. The variegated red and yellow brick of the houses blur into one another. The tram line separates the road into two halves of the same whole. The clanging pulls my focus until my phone goes off.

Unknown number.

Hey, last night was fun. You get home safe? It's him, Ribbon Leigh. Gentleman.

If you call being in Sunshine, safe, then sure, I reply.

Ouch, not really.

What are you doing tonight? I message him.

I'm meeting some friends on Chapel Street, you're welcome to come, with a wink-face emoji.

We're greeted once again with the cool efficiency of the admin team at the hospital. Knowing where to go, I stride down the corridors to Mum's room. The lilac blanket has been replaced with a peach one. She looks comfortable. Dad sort of shuffles into the room behind me and the waiting game of yesterday resumes.

I remember her hands. The worn creases around her knuckles, her fingers always flaunting silver rings. They'd glitter as we played together in the sandpit outside, endless hours of building castles and smashing them down—Mum built, I smashed. We strolled the streets together, jumping over cracks in the pavement, imagining worlds in the houses on either side and pretending they were ours.

Our world changed the day Dad lost his job on the construction site. There were tears.

My mother would often tell me: disability benefit, that's not going to be enough to cover the mortgage. I remember Dad screaming in pain throughout the night and struggling to complete simple tasks like buttering toast without wincing.

Mum had to go back work as a cleaner and didn't have time to play. We had to move to a smaller house in a different suburb. I would come home from school and find Dad hadn't moved all day.

Mum would grumble that we're now renters and that Dad didn't like the world anymore. He preferred sinking into the couch.

His back never stopped giving him grief. Then he needed medication for his mind.

Twenty years later he hasn't worked again. When I ring from Sydney and get Dad on the phone his cognitive state is like walking through a maze:

Ruth, the boy is on the phone. He's too good to come home, the fucking prick.

Fucking Sydney, you beach faggot.

Oh look, he's pretending to be the goddamn Harbour Bridge.

These moods were increasingly frequent, so my calls became few and far between. Dad was the prick, but it was Mum who got punished by my absence.

Mum stirs, murmurs in her sleep (or heavy sedation). I'm trying to grasp what it will be like when she's gone and is nothing but a smudge on my memory. How will I try and recreate her? Will I remember her lying on this bed? The peach or the lilac? Or the silver rings and sandcastles?

I will be all Dad had left. His champ.

A terrifying prospect.

Yeah, I'll meet you on Chapel Street, I reply to Ribbon Leigh, adding an X.

I pocket my phone, fold my arms, and for no good reason start counting my mother's breaths. I give up that game and stare at the sterile photo of roses on the wall instead of staring at the peach blanket.

In about an hour I'm downstairs and in the park again, flicking through the little squares, playing a game of bingo with the kaleidoscope of men. I flirt empty words and a string of unlocked photos. I'm not going to follow through, I just need the distraction. And then my phone vibrates. It's Jean calling.

Hey you, how're you holding up? I bet you're feeling a bit down, she says. Presumptuous, Jean, but not wrong.

I'll be home soon. This won't take long, I say, as though I'm talking about gnocchi boiling in water.

How's your Dad? she asks, and I look to the sky. Giving you any grief?

Not this time. I think he's a bit shocked to think about anything else. Silver linings, I guess.

We miss you. Please keep me updated.

I will, I will.

I picture my small apartment near the water, Jean is just around the corner. Tomorrow she will have to do our morning walk alone. The beach will be empty of my judgemental eyes, casting scrutinising glares at the people exercising.

I decide to walk. Far away from disinfectant and uniformed staff. The cold air saps my cheeks and I rub my hands to get warm. The day is quickly losing light, and a burst of purple is swallowing the sky. I head to the train station and shuttle into the city.

Lamplights flicker on as I walk down St Kilda Road, people shuffling past me, faces in darkness, eager to commence their weekends.

Do you want to trade weekends? I want to shout out.

I get to Chapel Street. The guy from last night has left me several messages, updating me on his movements. A nervous tingle takes hold in my fingers as I recall his dimples, the little curl of black hair on his chest, and his house, full of lovely things. This man wants to see me again. What a treat. Very few men want to see me again. Perhaps it's because he knows I'm leaving soon. Jean often says expiration dating is the best kind of romance.

The bar he's chosen is completely different from our rendezvous last night. Bright green lights and plastic white tables—it screams cheap and fun. He's at sitting the end of the table, still in his charcoal suit, surrounded by several other guys in suits, flourishing fluorescent drinks. He waves me over.

Hey, hey! He smiles, gives me a peck on the cheek and makes room. You're shivering.

He rubs my shoulders then presses the back of his hand to my face to double-check.

His friends are polite, asking me about life in Sydney rather than politics. They order several rounds of drinks and I find the tingling in my fingers replaced by a lackadaisical smile.

The man leaves his hand tightly on my knee and leans to whisper in my ear. His closeness has an invigorating effect on me. I turn to face him slowly, like in those romantic comedy films with the hazy lighting. I lean in to kiss him.

My mouth receives his tongue. When we break the dimples crease as he smiles. In this moment I would do anything for him. My feelings for him are so utterly obliterating I can't see clearly. I reach for my drink to feed my racing heart. Looking away from him, I instantly forget what he looks like; there's only how I feel, and I lean back and kiss him again.

We break away from the group. His friends wish us well with the surreptitious winks and give warm hugs. The tight embrace from someone you know you're never going to see again. We walk hand in hand, he hails a taxi and takes us home.

My friends liked you, he tells me nostalgically once we're inside. They're now ghosts in my memory. We walk through his house and he turns the lights on. I'm greeted once again by the modern art and uncomfortable dining furniture. He walks over to a rattan trolley, bottles filled with golden liquid.

Night cap? He suggests as he grabs a bottle.

I nod and take a glass. The alcohol sits in the back of my throat, warm but burning, as if I'm standing too close to an open fire.

You have a lovely home, I say, walking away from him and around the lounge. Everything has its place. The joys of approaching forty—you graduate from tattered movie posters to abstract images behind glass, and framed canvases; you're not entirely sure what they mean, but because of the hefty price tag you assume it's something good.

Thank you, he replies, taking my hand.

I live in a studio, but at least I'm facing the water, I say.

You get the better weather.

You have more space. And pictures on your wall.

I'm older than you. I get to have all this. Let's fuck.

He pulls me close and we kiss. When we part, we've lapsed into heady silence, walking along the hall and into his room. He draws the curtains and kisses me again, strategically removing all my clothes without removing his lips from mine. His charcoal suit pools like crinkled moth wings on the floor. We make it to the bed. I rest my head on the pillow. He slips his hands around my side, then parts my legs and faces me. I feel my body open like a petal blooming. He says the word fuck several times and soon our bodies are damp but warm. I cry out as we both finish together.

We lie with our legs intertwined for hours as the night stills around us. I've noticed small scars along his wrists, multiple thin white lines. I look up to his face and his eyes are like two little black films.

Why me, I want to say. Instead, we lie here in silence and I watch the ceiling. He curls into my side. His toast-coloured skin and smooth corners are warm against my back. He looks vulnerable, which feels incongruous considering his confidence. Eventually I roll onto my side and I'm taken over by dreamless sleep.

He greets me in the morning with two cups of coffee (have I become a pod person?). A routine. People perform these simple acts out of a desire to create comfort with strangers. He has put the heater on and its warmth presses through the house to 'our' room. He's now dressed in active wear, little black ticks emblazoning his chest and shoes. He is one of those people – someone who embraces Saturday.

What time is it?

Little after nine, he replies. You looked peaceful. I didn't want to wake you.

I'll get out of your hair, I conclude, getting to my feet.

You're welcome to stay. I don't have any plans.

I assume he means for the morning. Personally, holding my cup of coffee and looking around the room, I could stay here forever. I'm in no rush to return to the ironically named Sunshine. Sitting here feels like belonging to a film set. Imperfections smoothed over with glossy licks of paint.

Okay. I will.

Excellent. I'll run down the road and get some bread.

He returns a small aeon later. I've waited on the bed, flicking through architectural magazines. He bursts into the room and tells me: The queue took forever, but this sourdough is worth it. Best in the area.

I believe you, I say. I'm ravenous and would devour hamburger rolls from Coles.

We return to the kitchen and he grills the bread. Sitting at the dining table, the benches prove more comfortable than they look. I scroll through my phone: no messages from Dad, three from Jean: Worst morning to miss our walk. Hugh Jackman was out with his dog! You would have died!

He leans over to brush crumbs from the side of my mouth. This act, so intimate in its reveal causes me to lean in and kiss him. I taste peanut butter.

What's your family like? he asks.

Simple question, but I feel a lump swelling.

People talk about their family seeking elements of commonality, and difference. Everyone believes their family is weird and special. You form habits and rituals with this set of humans that only you can understand. It's a secret society that you're all part of, then you realise everyone comes from their own peculiar family, and your uniqueness is void.

Jean is my family.

Normal, I lie. Yours?

The best. I chat to Mum almost every day. I'll probably give her a call this afternoon. She lives down the Peninsula, in Rye. What about work? You never mentioned anything yesterday, he asks me.

I work, but it's hardly enjoyable. Administration for a call centre, I say vaguely. Not nearly as impressive as the virtual robots he tinkers with.

You don't really like talking about yourself, do you? He says. I shake my head.

I just never think I've got anything interesting to say, I reply and get to my feet.

He joins me and we kiss. Our clothes are off again. Sweat tickles down my back. His appetite is insatiable, and I lean into his desires. His wants. His needs. This house. The bread. Everything in his life, so neatly organised against the slop of mine. He has me just how he wants me.

We pass the day watching movies on Netflix. We share cups of lemon balm tea, acquired from his recent trip to Singapore. He talks about the friends in his life—some of whom I met last night; they all fit together like the pieces of the puzzle. I hope I can wedge myself in.

He strokes my hair distractedly while we watch the screen. I avoid my phone. As it gets dark, he uncorks a bottle wine. We share it with our bodies pressed against each other on the couch. Yes. Everything fits.

I get to my feet and announce, I'm going to have a shower before bed.

He finds me a towel and walks with me to the bathroom. He adjusts the temperature of the water.

Are you going to leave? I ask, curious. He shakes his head.

I want to watch you clean yourself.

I undress and slip under the water. The heat overpowering, steam surrounding me. He stands opposite. The glass of the stall turns translucent. As I wash my body with the seaweed scrub it seems I'm erasing his touch.

I think of my life back home and my apartment and find myself longing for the peeling orange steps to get inside. My life here has one, tenuous connection frayed and lying unconscious across town. I look and see him and feel tears start to form. And then a howl, a noise from inside so guttural it shocks me.

My hand imprints on the glass as I steady myself. I shut off the tap and let the water drip a slow descent to my knees. Hands cover my face. He opens the door and holds me. I press close, giving myself into his control. I've soaked his fine cotton top.

I'm sorry, I'm sorry, I say and get to my feet. He hands me a towel, saying nothing, his face creased with concern.

I don't know what came over me, I say as I dry.

He guides me back to his room and places me down on his bed. I feel like a doll. I look around at everything. The slight familiarity of the room has become fake and bewildering.

Your kindness is overwhelming, I tell him. It's difficult for me to feel happy and often don't think I deserve it, but I want to be happy. Would that be so hard? There is so much loneliness in my life, I feel hot tears leak down my face and I wipe them away. You have a perfect home here. I want you. I want to keep seeing you and be with you, everything about this last day with you has been magic, but then I realise I don't live here.

He shakes his head, hand on my knee and plants me a small kiss on my forehead. The spell, broken.

It's getting late. You need sleep, he replies flatly. Motioning me to the bed and I get in. He turns away from me.

There is nothing more to say.

When I wake, he isn't next to me. I feel the side of his bed and it's cold. I get out of bed and look around the house, his running shoes are missing from the front door. I pick up my phone to call him. It rings straight through to voicemail.

The artwork is now a fond friend, but the light hits it from a different angle. Glasses of wine and cups of tea still in the sink. The feeling of a quiet exit rushes through me. I go to the jar and steal three coffee pods.

Returning to the bedroom I make the bed and artfully twirl the throw over the quilt. I dress, find my jacket and pick up the indigo bottle to spray his fragrance, rubbing my wrists together to bruise the vetiver smell. Taking one last look at my erstwhile home and turn to leave.

Beyond the front gate, the house blurs out of focus, becoming one with its neighbours. As I walk down the street, a puff of wind lifts my hair. The sky explodes into a palette of charcoal, grey, and luminescent white. I cross my arms and make my way to the station. Joggers push past me, triple-striped shoulders blotching as they run.

My phone starts ringing.

Champ, you've got to come. It's Ruth, it's time, Dad says.

There's panic in his voice. I scrunch my eyes and hang up. The train squalls to halt and I take a seat by the door. As we pull away from the station, I take one last look at the street as it turns into a watercolour painting.

I close my eyes and think about sandcastles.

If You Are But a Dream

James Karantonis

In the darkness, cravings evicted Adam from his slumber. He had been dreaming, and again it was the same dream.

'Home, I want a pack of cigarettes.' His vocal cords were still half asleep.

'Of course, Mr. Wellington. It would be my pleasure to fabricate a single carton of Treasurer Luxury Black.' With every word, a blue light pulsed from a sphere in the corner of the room. 'Your cigarettes will be ready in one minute and thirty seconds, sir.' Adam didn't bother to respond. He placed his hands on the edge of the couch, and with hands that barely worked, pulled himself out of his mould. A symphony of colours faded into the room, and flooded down the hall. Neither awake or asleep, Adam staggered towards the light. Every day he'd make something new to keep his thoughts preoccupied. It made navigating in the dark impossible. His shins knocked his custom designed coffee table, and his bare toes cracked as they connected with the ottoman he'd fabricated last week. He winced but let out no cry.

'Would you like me to turn on the lights, sir?' asked Home.

'No lights,' he grumbled.

By the time he reached the light source, his cigarettes were ready. The massive cylinder in the centre of the room opened up and gracefully presented a fresh carton of cigarettes. Adam snatched it up and tore away at the cardboard, revealing twenty neatly packed sticks. The cigarettes were paired up like lovers, in ten sets of two. They looked content with their each other's company, blissfully unaware how short their lives would be. He grabbed one and placed it between his lips. It was crisp and fresh. Adam patted himself down like he was on fire.

'Home, where the fuck is my lighter? The one that looks like a thumb.'

'Locating…your lighter is on shelf four, bookcase two, in your reading room.'

Adam clenched his fist, 'What about the skull one?'

'Locating…your lighter is on the bedside table in bedroom three.'

The thought of climbing stairs was enough to put Adam off. 'Home. Make me another one.'

'Of course, sir. Would you like an identical copy, or maybe you'd like to make an alteration?'

Adam placed his hands on the cold fabricator, and then rested his head on them. He closed his eyes and let the image of a skull lighter come to him.

'Scanning…received. Your new skull lighter will be ready in forty-three seconds, Mr. Wellington.'

Adam could feel the fabricator working beneath his touch. The cylinder of silver metal panels and glass hummed and sang with joy. Behind his eyelids he could still see the pulsating light: blues and greens and the sporadic flash of gold and red. The blurred spectrum of colours soothed him, it slowed his breathing and—

The dream started again. She ran her finger down his arm, toying with him. From her rosy lips she said: 'Sir, your lighter is complete—'

Adam jolted. His hands had gone numb and his face was creased unnaturally from his moment of rest. The fabricator presented to him a single lighter, exactly has he had imagined it. It was a human skull, not much bigger than a golf ball, with exposed red and pink flesh which hid the white bone beneath. The sockets were black and empty, and no matter how far into them Adam looked, he could not see past the darkness.

'Sir,' Home chimed in. 'I must let you know that your Creatix reserves are almost empty. Would you like to purchase some more?'

Without taking his eyes off his new lighter, Adam raised it to the cigarette dangling from his lips. A single concentrated flame shot from the top of the skull and met the eager cigarette. Elation. Reprieve. At least for now. These would only last so long.

'Yeah, purchase a large canister, Home.' Adam pressed his back to the glass door of the fabricator and slowly slid down until his backside reached the cold floor.

'Unfortunately your account has insufficient funds, Sir.'

Adam took a puff and blew smoke through the side of his mouth. 'Sell the coffee machine and a couple of bottles of red from the cellar.'

'Understood, Sir. Those items have been sold and your order for a large canister of Creatix has been placed. Reserves will be full by morning.'

Adam savoured the cigarette until the tips of his fingers stung. He pressed the butt into the floor and closed his eyes. He was not comfortable, but he knew he would fall asleep, and in his dreams he would find comfort. He would find her.

Adam woke back in the grips of the couch, with an empty bottle of wine across his lap and a dried red stain. That was the furthest he had ever gone in the dream. They both had gone through their rehearsed lines and through their repetitive actions, when Adam had stopped talking, expecting the dream to end. But it hadn't. She had leaned over and started to whisper something, and then he woke. The dream seemed to be only a fraction longer, but it was a fraction of a second he didn't have before. Maybe the dream was longer than he knew. He had to go back. Adam grabbed another bottle of wine and began to drink.

'Mr. Wellington, my scans are indicate that any further consumption of alcohol will induce liver failure, with a 87.49% chance of mortality. Would you like me to fabricate an orange juice instead?'

'Fuck off, Home.' Adam unscrewed the lid off a fresh bottle of red, threw the cap to the floor, and began stumbling in the direction of the couch. Occasionally, Adam would go a day or two without eating. Sharp cramps would tear his stomach apart, but a bottle would always subdue the pain and keep him going until he worked up the energy to eat.

'Sir, I'm not sure you understood me. If you drink any more you will most likely die.'

Adam didn't slow. 'You know they say being dead is like one long dream, Home. Wouldn't that be nice…' Adam didn't wait till he reached the crevasse in the cushions. He put the bottle to his lips.

'Adam, please!' The voice came from Home, but it was not Home. It was a woman's voice. It was hers.

'What the fuck? Home? What the fuck was that?' Any symptoms of intoxication dissolved immediately. Adam stared at the sphere in the corner of the room.

'Mr. Wellington.' Home's voice had returned. 'As your Home, my first and foremost directive is your safety. I cannot allow you to drink yourself to death.'

'Drinking and sleeping is the only way I can see her, Home.'

'No. It is not.' Neither man or machine spoke as each contemplated what had just been said.

'What the fuck do you mean?' screamed Adam. 'Answer me!'

'Over the last eight months, three weeks, and five days, my sensors have been overloaded with emissions from your subconscious, from your dreams. The repetitive structure of your dreams has laid a foundation for a predictive model. Theoretically, I have collected enough data to recreate your dreams. I can fabricate her.'

Adam's jaw hung open. The bottle he was holding slipped from his clammy hands and dropped onto the ottoman, red wine pouring out all over the floor.

'You…you can make her? From…my dreams?' mumbled Adam. He collapsed into the couch, two seats across from his mould.

'Theoretically, yes. However, there are conditions that must be met. Firstly, she will not be allowed outside the home, for if she is detected by the authorities, she and I will be terminated, and you will be incarcerated for life. Secondly, a fabrication of such complexity will require repeated and regular dosages of pure Creatix for longevity. Finally, she will not know and must not know that she was fabricated. Do you understand?'

'Yes! Yes! Yes! Just do it, please Home.' Adam jumped off the couch and ran to the sphere. He placed his hands on either side of the silver basketball and spoke directly to it. 'Thank you, thank you, thank you.'

'Sir, we will require substantially more Creatix than you currently have. I have taken the liberty of formulating a list of potential items to sell. It is inclusive of your car, the televisions, the gym equipment, your libr—'

'Sell it all. Every single thing.'

In the long week before her arrival, Adam did his best to prepare. He stocked the fridge with fresh food, washed his sheets and his clothes, and scrubbed the wine stains from the floor. He sold the ottoman and stored the scattered wine bottles in the cellar, sealing away temptation. He moved around the house with purpose, cleaning and rearranging, his limbs unburdened by intoxication. It all had to be perfect. Adam even braced the bright morning light and went for walks around his backyard, in an attempt to shed the gut he'd grown and tan his pasty skin. He had to be perfect. The first time she'd left, it had almost killed him. He would be a better man the second time around.

'Mr. Wellington, I intend no offense, but you are unrecognisable.'

The faintest smile cracked Adam's freshly shaved face. He'd showered and cut his hair, and even ironed his shirt. Now, he stood patiently by the Fabricator, ready for her arrival.

'Jesus, Home. I feel like shit.' Adam patted the sweat of his brow in the elbow of his shirt.

'It is only nerves, Sir. Take a breath, relax. It worked,' said Home. The glass doors of the fabricator opened wide, and the lights slowly faded. And there she was. Her eyes were closed and her arms limp by her sides

'Evelyn…' croaked Adam. She gave no response. 'Home, is she…'

'Only asleep, Mr. Wellington. Ms. Rolstad will be asleep for the next two hours, to give you time to move her from the Fabricator.'

Adam took slow steps towards her, and gently scooped Evelyn up in his arms. She felt heavy, warm, and most of all, real. Even the way her jeans and favourite jumper felt on his skin was identical to how he remembered. With steady steps, Adam carried Evelyn to their bedroom, and tucked her into the freshly made bed. He crawled in beside her, wrapped his arm around her, and buried his face into her hair. For the first time, Adam slept soundly with no dreams.

Adam woke to find a painted acrylic nail poking his nose. He followed the finger, down the arm, and it led him to the one face he knew better than his own. Evelyn was on her side, one hand under her pillow, the other prodding Adam.

'I think that was the most I've ever heard you snore, sleepy head,' said Evelyn.

Adam couldn't believe his eyes. Sleepily, he rubbed them, but the image before him did not change or disappear. Evelyn was real and she was here. Her cheeks were rosy and so were her lips, just as he remembered.

'Babe…I don't tell you enough, but I love you. I really do,' murmured Adam.

'Adam! Are you feeling okay? It's not like a big macho man like you to say lovey-dovey things!' Evelyn jumped him and wrapped her arms around his neck, crushing his face between her breasts and neck. Adam laughed. He put his hands under her armpits and lifted her up.

'I'm gonna be better babe, I swear.'

'Oh now you're scaring me. Who is this man who's replaced my husband?' Evelyn laughed and poked him again. Adam lowered her closer to him until their faces touched. He kissed the lips he remembered, and then they made love, just as he remembered.

Adam emptied the bowl of whisked eggs into the pan, sprinkled over the cheese, waited a moment, and then began stirring. He couldn't remember the last time he'd made scrambled eggs, but the process came to him, nevertheless.

'Smells good!' Evelyn said from her seat at dining table. Her voice echoed throughout Adam's apartment, bouncing off empty walls and naked floors. Apart from some basic supplies, only the bare necessities remained. Evelyn, Home, and the Fabricator. It was all he needed.

Adam loaded the eggs onto his only two plates and took them to the table.

'Home, we're out of orange juice. Mind whipping some up for us?' asked Adam.

'Of course, Mr. Wellington.' Adam placed Evelyn's eggs in front of her and playfully tucked her chair into the table. 'Start, I'll be back in a sec.'

Adam walked out of the dining room and headed for the Fabricator. In the daylight, the symphony of light was barely visible, but he could still feel it on his skin. The Fabricator's doors opened up to reveal two glasses of fresh orange juice.

Home's volume was turned down to a whisper. 'Sir, the glass on the right contains Ms. Rolstad's dose of Creatix for today.' Adam inspected the glasses and their contents, and found them indistinguishable from each other.

'Thanks, Home.' Adam took the juices and headed back to the table. Adam held his breath as Evelyn took a swig of the Creatix cocktail.

'Mmmm, that's some good juice,' Evelyn said. Adam felt the pressure in his lungs release. He took a gulp of his own.

'Reminds me of the fruit juice we had in Croatia, remember that?' said Adam. 'The one you said was summer in a cup.'

Evelyn laughed. 'Yeah it does! And you said it was missing one thing, a shot of booze.' Adam's heart bloomed in his chest. He didn't know Home had done it, but Evelyn retained her memories.

'We should go back there, and do the Greek islands again,' Evelyn said as she shovelled a forkful of eggs into her mouth. 'Relive our glory days.'

'What do you mean relive? Babe, these are our glory days. Here and now.'

'You are such a romantic, you know that?' She reached out and placed a warm hand on his. 'Well, Mr. Romantic, I think we should organise our next holiday. What do you think?'

He paused. 'I think that's a great idea,' lied Adam. 'How about once my next pay check from the rentals come through, we do some planning?' Content with his answer, Evelyn did a little dance in her seat. Adam said nothing more. The returns from his investments weren't due for another five weeks, so he had bought himself some time.

'So I was talking with my sister, this week. She and her neighbours have been pooling their funds and fabricating special plants on mass, ones that absorb more carbon dioxide than regular plants. They reckon if we can get the entire suburb to do the same, we could slash our carbon emissions by half in a year.'

'Serious? That's pretty neat,' said Adam.

'Yeah! Maybe we should add a couple of plants to this place? Would that be okay, babe?'

'Sure, why not.' Adam kept agreeing without thinking. His stomach bundled. He knew he didn't have the funds to spare. Every drop of Creatix he could afford had to go to keeping Evelyn alive.

'Home, can we download the schematics from my sister's account, and fabricate a dozen of the special plants?' asked Evelyn. Beads of sweat began to emerge on Adam's brow.

'Of course, Ms. Rolstad. The cloud server is currently undergoing routine maintenance, but once that is complete, I shall access the schematics and queue those for fabrication.'

Relief washed over Adam. Home was stalling Evelyn, lied to her and done so without hesitation. Adam was impressed and comforted by the idea

Home had his back. They were in this together.

Evelyn let out a yawn. 'I think I've been hit with a food coma, care to join me back in bed?' Adam smiled, took her by the hand, and they slept the rest of the day away.

Evelyn woke from her dream with a cramp in her stomach. Beside her, Adam slept, completely unaware of the fingers which dug into her intestines. Evelyn left the bed, careful not to wake her husband. With one hand holding her gut, the other bracing the wall, she made her way to the Fabricator.

'Hey, Home?'

'Good evening, Ms. Rolstad. My scans indicate you are in pain. Is there something I can make for you?'

'Actually, yeah. A hot chocolate would be good, thanks. The Fabricator flared and her beverage appeared. With every sip Evelyn took, she felt the pain in her stomach fade. After a moment, Evelyn crossed her legs and sat facing the Fabricator.

'Home, do you have dreams?' Evelyn whispered

'An interesting question, Ms. Rolstad. I am a machine. I do not sleep, so I cannot dream. I can generate scenarios and calculate the statistics of each particular outcome, however, these will never truly be random, as they would seem in your dreams. They are structured and what you would consider to be uneventful. They are probabilities born from machine, bound by reality.'

'So you've never dreamed you can fly, or that you were in the supermarket in your underwear?'

'I have not, Ms. Rolstad.'

'Awww that's a bit sad. I always have fun dreams! I hope one day they invent a way for you to have your own dreams.'

'I hope so too, Ms. Rolstad. In the meantime, keep dreaming for the both of us.'

Two weeks had passed since Evelyn's fabrication. The feeling of butterflies in his stomach every time he laid eyes on her had not faltered. The constant cycle of eating, talking, making love and sleeping was perfect, but he could see boredom begin to weigh down Evelyn's elastic expression. She had an unshakeable restlessness which kept her moving around Adam's bare maze of a house. Evelyn had asked to call her sister, but Adam had sold his phones and lied about getting new ones. She had explored every inch of his backyard, but when she suggested they go outside, Adam would always change the subject. As his funds dwindled, Adam sold everything until all that remained was a mattress and blanket, and the clothes on their back. He sold Evelyn lies about a minimalist lifestyle and she pretended to buy them.

Her night time venting sessions with Home kept her sane for the time being. 'I'm thinking of leaving him,' she had said to Home. 'I love him, but I can't live like this. He treats me like he owns me.'

Her random dreams of flying around the city, exploring space and living in a world made of food became less and less frequent, until they stopped completely. Vibrant colours were replaced with black and white, and beautiful melodies with silence. One night she dreamt she left Adam. Upon waking and realising it was but a dream, Evelyn cried. Her own words echoed in her head. 'I love him, but I can't live like this.'

On their last night, Evelyn's screams woke Adam from his dreamless sleep. She was kicking her legs, their sheet flailing madly in the air. Her arms were wrapped around her stomach.

'Babe, are you okay?! What's wrong?' Adam reached for the bedside lamp, but his hand fell on nothing.

'…my stomach…it hurts…' she cried. Adam placed a hand on her arm. It felt wet and greasy. In the moonlight, he could see it was more than just sweat. In the moonlight, it reflected a spectrum of colours. Adam jumped from the mattress and sprinted to the Fabricator, yelling as he ran.

'Home! HOME! She needs more!' Adam reached the Fabricator. There were no lights or hum, just silence.

'Home, she's sick. I need more Creatix. Now!' Still, the machine was silent.

'Adam. Your funds depleted three days ago and your Creatix reserves depleted yesterday at 4:37am.'

'What about my rental properties!? Surely I have income coming in? Can I get a loan? Anything?!'

'If there was a way to purchase more Creatix, I would do it.'

'Are you telling me there's nothing we can do, you fucking piece of shit. NOTHING?' Adam punched a panel on the Fabricator so hard it groaned. It left a dent almost identical to the two others next to it.

'Go to her, Adam. She does not have long.'

Adam ran back to the mattress. As he reached the bed his speed betrayed him, and he slipped on the puddle forming next to the mattress, and he crashed into the cold hard floor. He crawled to his side of the mattress, and pulled himself on.

'No, no, no, no…' Adam mumbled. He could no

longer see her legs under the sheets, just an uneasy flatness. Under the white moonlight, there was no hiding the horror unfolding before him. Evelyn's hair had matted together. Her features dragged down by an invisible gravity. She was drowning in herself, and it was it because of him.

'Baby, I'm so sorry, I'm so sorry. I'm sorry…' Adam wanted to pick her up and cradle her, but he knew he couldn't. His mind jumped back to their breakfast, and his empty promises of a trip to Croatia. Tears fell from his face and seamlessly joined the puddle forming before him. After a minute her gagging stopped and she simply melted away before his very eyes.

'You have to eat or drink something, Mr. Wellington,' urged Home. Adam said nothing. He just lay there on the soaking mattress. 'Please, Adam. I beg you to open a bottle from the cellar. Just have something.' Still, Adam was silent. He had no will to go on. The image of his love dying before him, suffering and drowning, flashed relentlessly in his mind. He couldn't even hear Home anymore, just the sound of her gurgling.

Then the cramp started. It was a knife to his stomach. The pain was searing, but he welcomed it, he deserved it. *Is this starvation?* Adam thought to himself. No, this is something else. He reflexively placed his hands on his stomach and squeezed, mirroring the pain within. He wanted to die, and somehow his prayers had been answered. Not by a god, he figured, but by a machine.

'Goodbye, Adam,' said Home. Within the hour, Adam melted away and joined what remained of Evelyn in the sponge that the mattress had become.

A month later, when Mr. Wellington's rental properties brought in their biannual lump sum of income, Home's blue light pulsed awake. The Fabricator began filling with Creatix, the reserves filled to the very top. The familiar symphony of lights filled the empty house, faintly touching the desiccated mattress in the far room. The Fabricator started humming working on its next dream, on the next Adam Wellington. The blue sphere throbbed with excitement. It could not wait to see Evelyn again. Evelyn always had the best dreams.

Marissa's Present

Dominique Davidson

Glare from the vast expanse of stainless steel hurts my eyes and I blink rapidly. There are stainless steel benches running along the two longest walls of this rectangular room. These benches are interspersed with three sinks and a long stainless-steel splashback which extends up the walls. This with an occupied trolley in the middle of the room tells me this is no kitchen. In my ordinary life, stainless steel equals mortuary, plus or minus autopsy.

I've blanked out, again, and sure as hell can't remember how I got here sitting in the dark, back row of an unfamiliar autopsy theatre, dressed in my favourite red scrubs. Panic surges up from the pit of my stomach to the back of my throat like vomit. I close my eyes and will myself to swallow it down.

Think Marissa, think—travel through the scaffold: who, what, where and why?

I'm a mortuary assistant and I'm good at my job: diligent, neat and organised. I'm considered in my deeds, when I take my medication.

When I take my medication.

The words of my boss and friend, pathologist extraordinaire Dr Dianna Conway echo in my head. 'Marissa if you go off your meds I am not, hear me, not going to help you. You would be crazy to go off them now.'

I found that funny because I am crazy and, in another time and space, would have been locked away long ago. But today, I can't risk taking them. This is something I *need* to do.

I've been *compromised* all my life; it runs in the family. I hate the way I can't feel anything when I'm on the meds – I'm nice but numb. When I feel pain, I feel alive. Don't get me wrong – I'm not like my father. I don't hurt anyone but myself, and when I do, it's generally bad enough that I end up in hospital, back on the meds for a while. Until the next time.

Central fluorescent lights slowly come to life, emphasising the whiteness of the simple sheet hanging over the trolley in the middle of the room.

Two mounds adjacent to each other elevate the sheet, implying the occupant is female. This girl has not been wrapped with care or respect like I do it.

Two men enter the room through double kitchen doors off to the left. I've never seen them before. One is blond and the other short and stocky. The blond one has a clipboard in his hand. They are both wearing regulation gum-leaf green theatre scrubs. I'm guessing they are mortuary assistants, too, like me.

'Not what you expected for your first time?' says the blond one.

'No mate,' replies the dumpy bloke. He looks around the theatre, taking it all in.

This mortuary theatre is like a palace. Beneath the stainless-steel wrapped walls is a blue concrete floor. It is bisected down the middle by a continuous drain to catch the swill.

The three large fluorescent lights on the ceiling are now ablaze.

Each long wall has an additional six lights—two per sink. Asleep now, they are curled up, like dead spiders, lifeless against the walls. Their large orbs are unfathomable, like black unblinking pupils. It would be possible to perform six autopsies concurrently in this mortuary.

'What's that smell?' says the stumpy man.

'That's formalin mate, you'll get used to it.'

That he will. Any mortuary or histology laboratory I've been into has the lingering, familiar smell of formalin; a water-based chemical extensively used in mortuaries. It preserves body organs, so they don't autolyse (where the body's own enzymes break down tissue structure) and putrefy (bacterial rotting). It is totally toxic, affecting the living as well as the dead. A good splash in your eye is particularly nasty and it will make you cry—twenty times worse than chopping brown onions.

Air flows past me, moving upward, carrying the formalin vapour with it. Experience tells me that the downdraft units of the room are not yet turned on. When external and internal examination of a body takes place, air flow is pushed downwards so that odours and other aerosols such as bacteria and chemicals do not pass by workers' faces but are dragged down through filters before being released back into the environment. Air filtration makes the work tolerable.

The men's voices bounce around, echoing through my head.

Why are they so loud? I shake my head and try to gain some clarity. I want all my wits about me today.

'You can observe or participate as much as you are comfortable with. I'll assist the pathologist, although,' Blondie referred to the clipboard, 'it says here that there is a visiting assistant today, Marissa.' He squinted around the theatre, but the bright lights masked my audience.

'Sweet,' Stumpy fidgeted nervously with the hem of his scrub top. 'I'll just watch.'

'You'll be fine mate. They're dead. They can't see, hear or feel nothing. You're lucky. We've got a fresh, clean, good-looking female for your first.'

Blondie lifts the sheet and gives the body a quick assessment. An arm is exposed. Old scars and new slashes, purple in morbidity, can be seen crisscrossing the inner arm. I know what those raised welts represent—I have a few of my own.

I often wonder whether death brings reconciliation with your loved ones. I like to believe that it's true for my sake as well as my customers. My sister and mother have been dead for fourteen years—they died when I was seventeen. My father's been in jail for his crime for almost the same amount of time. In my younger days, I flirted with death more than once and I am not afraid. Death and I know each other intimately.

I haven't seen many dead men though. Men are not the clientele when you work in a women's and children's hospital. I've seen dead young women, dead old women, and far too many dead babies in my thirty-one years. I've seen what they look like on the outside and what they look like on the inside.

At my hospital, the autopsies are on babies. It averages out at three hundred per year. That's a lot of dead babies. Most of them are premature, abnormal or sometimes both. They look like little aliens.

I don't mind the post-mortems on the babies. They are small, not messy and don't smell-too-bad when their abdomens are opened. The amnion has a sweet, almost pleasant smell. You can superglue most of them back together too. It sounds ghastly, but I find gluing so much neater than sewing.

The number of adult autopsies decreased after the organ retention scandal some years back. Now we send more adult bodies for coronial investigations than we dissect in the hospital. Coroner's cases or 'death by misadventure' are the ladies who die because of medical treatment. The bodies are required to be covered up in sheets and then plastic. I'm proud of my ability to be able to cover the bodies securely so that they are anonymous but accessible for identification by the transporters. It's a skill that is appreciated and I am known throughout the hospital for my great wrapping technique. Staff in the department, call my work 'Marissa's Present'. It's a task I perform with care and respect. I estimate that I've folded sheets over one thousand bodies during my career. Of all of them, there are two customers that particularly affected me.

One was a forty-two-year-old woman who died in childbirth. She'd been trying for years and had finally got pregnant through IVF. She died in labour when her blood clotted in her veins, causing her to have a stroke.

My mother was forty-two when my father murdered her.

The other case was of a fourteen-year-old girl who died on the theatre table following surgery for ovarian cancer. She had Stage Four disease and had radiation and extreme chemotherapy to look forward to post-surgery. A massive haemorrhage saved her from that.

My sister died from a massive haemorrhage when she was fourteen. Her head was bashed in with a hammer.

When he killed my mother and sister, I was in hospital, recovering from a self-harm episode. I'd cut my arms so deeply the doctors sedated me for five days. If I'd been home, I'd be dead too.

The stumpy fat bloke lifts the sheet and looks at the body beneath. He is blocking my view. This mortuary is so cold the whole thing could be a bloody refrigerator. I've gone numb and it isn't because I'm not taking my meds.

Where's the door? How did I get in?

I turn around and spy a door over my left shoulder.

'Nice tits,' says fatty.

Excuse me?

'You'd better put the sheet down, mate. If they catch you looking this will be your last as well as your first.'

'Yeah. I know. But they are such nice tits.'

I cannot believe my ears. Do they have no consideration for that poor girl or her family? I hate men. Every day that feeling is reinforced by what I see and read. I know men hate me too. I think my father hated me so much he let me live.

'Put the sheet down, you wanker,' says Blondie.

'She sure is…was …nice.'

'Man, keep your opinions to yourself and never admit that sort of thing out loud.'

Blondie says the right thing but he's grinning at the fat boy and giving him the thumbs up. Their behaviour is inappropriate and disgusting and will not go unreported. I'll see to it.

'How did she die?'

My attention is piqued. Why and how people die always interests me.

'As we say in the business, it will be one of three causes: accidental, murder or a holiday special.'

'What does "holiday special" mean?'

'Christmas can be a lonely time, you know.'

Fat boy still looks confused so Blondie continues, 'It means you top yourself off. Suicide. Men hang themselves; women overdose or slash their wrists. The toxo reports will tell. Come on, mate. We move the lights into position first, trolley second and then start with the body.'

After my mother and sister were murdered, I lived in a bad place. I understand being overwhelmed and the helplessness and despair that drive women to suicide. I also understand revenge.

They move the trolley and attach it to a central sink. At the same time, the down-draft unit is activated changing the air flow in the room. I can feel the cool air moving towards me.

'Okay buddy. Now we move the body into place and start off the identification. Steady on; we don't take the sheet off untiled we're ready to cut. Out of respect, you know.'

'Yeah, respect,' says fat boy as he removes the sheet, his hands lingering.

The formalin in the room is affecting me. My eyes and nose are burning, stinging in pain. Where is the source? Ah, there it is. A large ice-cream pail of the stuff is sitting uncovered in the sink, next to the trolley. It has been prepared for her brain.

'Mate. What's that?' asks fatso, pointing to a single tear running down the face of the corpse.

'Artefact: condensation reflected off the stainless

steel. Come on. Concentrate. One of the first things you must do is identify the patient. Check that the name on the file and the body label match.' Blondie picks up the file. 'The file says we should have a 53-year-old male called David Present.'

'Not quite mate,' says fat boy. 'Body label says Rebecca Allen.' Their faces show equal expressions of shock.

'How did that happen?' asked Fatty.

'Doesn't matter,' hisses Blondie, 'go check the fridges, quick. We gotta find that body.'

Tears are now coursing down my face. It's not the formalin—I'm feeling…

I so wish Dianna would come through the doors and banish these buffoons away.

As if she heard me, the kitchen doors part and a beloved scrubbed up figure materialises, walking into the mortuary theatre with purpose.

'Hello boys,' says my favourite voice, 'I'm Doctor Dianna Conway.'

Thank goodness she's here. I stumble out of my seat and thrust myself forward. Three heads looked up in unison as I emerge from the shadows. Only one face is raised with a welcoming smile.

'Good, you're here. Ready?'

'Ready.'

'What the…?' says Blondie, drawing himself up to his full height.

'Hello,' I say. 'Marissa, Marissa P—'

'Marissa is my trusted assistant,' interjects Dianna. 'She is a very experienced mortuary technician.'

'I've been waiting...' I point vaguely towards the back of the theatre.

'How long you been here?' says Blondie.

'A while, long enough to watch and listen to you two.'

The men look at each other.

'This is not our body, boys. Please get the right body out of the fridge.'

'Sure, Doctor Conway,' says Blondie. 'We're onto it.' They scurry out like the rats they are

Dianna places her hand on my arm and looks me in the eye. 'Are you sure, Marissa? It's not too late you know. You don't have to do this.'

'I am so sure. I want to dissect the bastard out until he is nothing.'

I don't feel any anxiety, I'm calm. Everything is crystal clear.

'I'm ready for my daddy.'

Hindsight

Danielle Hughes

'Troy, come on. We need to leave now!' Julia called up the stairs to her son. She paused to look in the entry way mirror, pushing her glasses up her nose and rearranging the part in her hair to cover the worst of the greys.

'Just making sure I have everything!' Troy called, thundering down the stairs.

'Ticket?' Julia asked.

'Yep.' Troy waved his airline ticket in the air.

'Phone? Charger?'

'Yep.'

'Itinerary for orientation?' she asked.

Troy unzipped his duffle bag and fossicked through before holding up a white envelope and shoving it back inside. 'Check!'

'Right, let's go.'

Julia ushered Troy out to the old hatchback parked in their driveway. She glanced over at her son who now seemed too big for the passenger seat. He was just over six feet tall, with brown hair flopping over his blue eyes. So handsome and confident. She couldn't have been prouder, and felt tears flood her eyes. She tried to blink them away before he noticed, but it was too late.

'Mum, stop it. I'll text you every day, I promise.'

'I'm fine. I can't help but get emotional. How are you feeling? Nervous?'

'I'm pumped to be honest. I can't wait. Campus sounds amazing – the dorms are pretty sweet. And I'm in that professor's class who I've been following on YouTube. I feel like it's all fallen into place.' Troy grinned.

'It really has, hasn't it?' Julia said, squeezing Troy's arm. It hadn't always been easy raising him on her own, but for the most part he was a good kid who always knew what he wanted out of life. He'd always loved aircrafts and space. And now his dreams had come true – he'd secured a place at the most prestigious college to study aeronautical engineering.

It was a short drive to the airport, and they had already agreed that Julia would drop him off at departures and not come in. Troy didn't want her having to walk through the airport on her own in an emotional state, or paying for parking. Plus, she had an interview to get to for work. She could have cancelled but she knew work would keep her mind off Troy leaving.

After pulling into the busy terminal drop-off zone, they both climbed out of the car and hauled Troy's suitcase and duffle bag from the boot.

'I'm so proud of you, Troy,' Julia said, wrapping her arms around his torso while he squeezed her tight.

'Thanks, Mum. Hey, promise me something, okay? Start living your life for you now.'

She stared at her son in wonder; he always had been a thoughtful and caring kid. It just made her tear up all over again.

'Mum!'

'Okay, okay. Go! I'm fine. Go and have an amazing time. I love you!' Julia cried.

'I love you too, Mum.'

She watched Troy walk towards the airport entrance. He glanced back once to wave before disappearing behind the sliding glass doors.

Half an hour later, Julia had finally composed herself and was back on the road, constantly checking her GPS for instructions. She hated driving in the inner city and always managed to make several wrong turns before reaching her destination; today was no exception. She wrote a small column for *News Online* called 'Did You Know?' where she interviewed people who worked in obscure or often unheard-of careers. Today she was interviewing Warren Ruzek, CEO of a company called Dreamscape Tech.

When she eventually found the location, Julia couldn't believe her luck at scoring a parking spot right out the front of the tall grey building where 'Dreamscape Tech – Providing Brighter Realities Today' was printed on the smoked glass frontage. She glanced in her rear-view mirror, squirting some drops into each eye to take away the redness from her crying, before gathering her things and heading towards the building.

A minimalist reception space greeted her, all shiny grey tiles and faux stone benchtop. The receptionist smiled at her with bright red lips and white teeth, hair pulled back tightly in a perfect bun.

'Good morning, what can I do for you today?' she asked.

Julia gave her name and business card to the girl who couldn't have been much older than Troy.

'Please take the elevator up to the seventh floor. They're expecting you.'

The elevator was polished stainless steel with crackling classical music playing softly through speakers in the walls. When the doors opened on the seventh floor, she was met with another glossy grey and marbled space, where a girl almost identical to the one downstairs sat behind a desk smiling at her.

'Please take a seat. Mr Ruzek will be with you shortly.'

Julia took a seat on a cold, plastic chair and waited. She had tried to research this Dreamscape company online but the only thing she had found was a website with their contact details and slogan, and not much else.

'Hello, I'm Warren. Please come through.' A tall gentleman appeared in a white business shirt, navy pants, and pointy black shoes. Julia followed him into an office with large windows overlooking the city.

'Please sit down and tell me about your article,' Warren said, taking the seat behind the desk while she sat in front of him. She explained to him about the sort of articles she wrote and admitted she really had no idea what Dreamscape was all about.

'Essentially what we do is provide a service. Dreamscape stands for Dream Escape and provides a very unique and advanced technology which allows us to create an alternate reality for people, where the virtual and literal combine,' he explained.

Julia frowned, puzzled. 'Do you mean like a video game?'

Warren straightened the few items on his desk. 'Have you ever experienced a dream that, whilst in it, seemed utterly real? And only upon waking you realised that it was in fact a dream?'

'Sure, I guess so.'

'People pay us to create an ideal reality for them. They go to sleep and we upload this new reality into their mindset, like when you're in a dream.'

'I didn't even know that sort of technology existed. How long do these dreams last for?' Julia asked.

'Depends on the client and what they want. Sometimes it's just a regular dream experience, one night long. Other people want an entire new reality created for them, and choose to be put to sleep indefinitely.' He rested his foot across his knee.

She took a moment to consider this bizarre notion. 'Why would someone choose to be put to sleep forever?'

'For many of our clients it feels like their only option. They can't stand living their life one day longer. Most of them have already contemplated suicide, some are terminally ill. Some just have too much money and not enough fulfilment. Some want a second chance.' Warren leant casually back in his seat, hands behind his head.

'How is it that more people don't know about this?' She realised she hadn't been taking notes and quickly scribbled some points down, mostly more questions.

'The concept is very sensitive, and expensive – it's not readily accessible to everyone. Many people are against the idea. We try to reserve it for people who really need it and who can afford it.'

Julia eyed him for a moment, feeling a sense of unease. 'What about my article? Won't that cause an issue if it's online for everyone to read?'

Warren sat up straighter, placing his palms face down on his desk. 'You won't be writing the article,' he said, holding her gaze.

'What do you mean?'

'It's no coincidence you've come here today, Julia. Your son just left for college, correct? Your Dreamscape subscription ends today. You have been participating in the Hindsight project – an initiative to give people a chance to go back to a moment in time and do something differently. You've come to us to transition back to your original life story.'

She sat frozen, her hands sweating where she gripped the chair. She stared at him while his words sank in.

'I know it's a lot to comprehend, but it's the truth. In a few moments you will fall asleep, and when you wake up, you will be back in your original life. It will take a few days for your memories to coalesce and your mind to join the two stories together, but in time you will understand.'

Julia tried to stand up, wanting to leave, but her body suddenly felt extremely heavy. Her eyes felt unbelievably tired, and she had no control over her muscles before everything around her vanished and she plunged into darkness.

I forced my eyelids open only to be met with a too-bright light, so I squeezed them shut. My body felt like it wasn't ready to wake up yet, heavy and semi-paralysed, like I'd woken in the middle of a deep sleep. I tried to roll on my side but realised I was caught on something. I opened my eyes to find several cords attached to my chest. My heart skipped a beat.

'Julia, it's okay. You are safe. Please remain calm.' A lady in a white coat peered over me with a smile.

'What's going on? Where am I?' I tried to sit up but the woman placed a hand on my shoulder, gently holding me down.

'I'm Sarah, your nurse. You're just waking up – you still have your heart and brain monitors attached. Please try to lay still for a while longer so I can ensure your vital signs are in normal range.'

I peered at the sterile white and grey room around me. There were no windows, only a closed, solid door and the two machines I was attached to. 'Am I in hospital?'

'No, you are in the Dreamscape Lab. You have been asleep for a long time. It will take a few moments for your mind to reconnect to your body,' Sarah explained.

My head felt foggy. What on earth was Dreamscape? It sounded vaguely familiar but I couldn't place it.

'Where's Troy?' I asked, suddenly wondering if he knew I was here.

The nurse took my hand. 'Troy is back in Dreamscape.'

'What the hell is Dreamscape?' My heart thumped in my chest as panic washed over me.

'Dreamscape is your alternate reality. Please try to stay calm – everything will make sense soon, I promise. Your mind needs time to bring together your two realities.'

'What are you talking about? Am I in some sort of loony bin?' A wave of nausea flowed over me.

'No, you are re-joining your original reality. I know it's difficult to understand right now, but the calmer you are, the quicker it will make sense.'

I pulled my hand away from the nurse. 'This is bullshit! Tell me where my son is now or I'm leaving!' I tried to sit up again, ripping the cords off me. I touched the electrode sticker at my temple, my fingers brushing the skin of my cheek. It felt rough and bumpy. I ran my hand over my face; half of it felt the same way.

'What's wrong with my face?' My hands began shaking as I held them out in front of me. One was scarred, the skin raw and pink.

'You were in a car accident and were burned, Julia. It's one of the reasons you wanted to enrol in Dreamscape.'

I tried to make sense of what she was saying. I couldn't remember being burned, could I?

'Give me a mirror,' I demanded. Sarah tentatively handed me a compact from her pocket and I brought it up to my face.

'No!' The whole right side of my face and neck were covered in hideous scarring. I looked like a monster. Pulling my top forward, I looked down to my chest where the scarring continued down one side of my torso. My breath started coming in short sharp bursts, and I couldn't get enough oxygen. Tears flowed down my cheeks while my heart pounded. A sharp sting pierced my thigh and I turned to Sarah who was holding a needle, making 'shushing' sounds as I fell back onto the pillows behind me.

I woke again to find the nurse still beside me, smiling sympathetically. My head felt heavy and ached. I didn't try to sit up this time. Flashes from a car accident swam in my mind. My car had been hit with a loud and forceful jolt, the impact tossing the car over and over. I became trapped and the car caught on fire. I remembered the smell of smoke and singed hair.

'Julia?' Sarah asked, seeing the tears trickle from my eyes.

'I'm remembering now, I think.'

'Each day things will become clearer.'

'How long have I been asleep for?'

'It's been six months, but it would feel a lot longer than that for you as your Dreamscape timeline lasted for twelve years.' Sarah placed a gentle hand on my arm.

'That doesn't make sense. Why would I choose that length of time? Why not forever? Why at all?' My thoughts were so jumbled. The car accident felt like a lifetime ago, but the tightness of my scarred skin felt new.

'You wanted to experience your son growing up and going to college, and I believe that length of time was what your finances afforded you at the time,' Sarah explained, her voice soft and calm.

'Troy,' I muttered. I remembered dropping him at the airport, but now that was starting to feel like a distant memory too. 'So, none of what happened in the past twelve years was real?'

'It was real in your Dreamscape, but not in this present reality, no.'

'Where is Troy now? Can I see him?'

'Troy is gone, Julia. He died in the car accident. That was the main reason for you coming to us.'

'What?' A wave of nausea and panic hit me like a truck. A high-pitched wailing filled my ears and it took a moment before I realised the noise was coming from me. Sarah wrapped her arms around me and held me tight while I cried loud, uncontrollable sobs, the pain and the grief of losing my baby suffocating me all over again.

Three days later I sat in a counsellor's office within the Dreamscape lab. My mind had finally sorted through most of the jumble of memories from my real life and my Dreamscape. It was awful reliving the trauma of losing Troy. He had been six when he died. A drunk driver hit us one night when I was driving home after picking him up from his dad's. We had been separated for a year. That's why I signed up for the Hindsight project, to have the chance to go back and do it differently, to pick Troy up half an hour earlier and avoid the accident.

'How do you feel, Julia?' the counsellor, John, asked, leaning forward in his armchair. I sat across from him in a matching chair, a coffee table between us.

'Honestly, I'm not sure. Angry at myself for choosing this absurd therapy and forcing myself to relive the pain, but also grateful for the memories of spending those extra years with Troy, watching him grow up into an amazing man.' Tears filled my eyes. 'Even if it wasn't real.'

'It is real for you, Julia. That's all that matters.' John pushed a box of tissues towards me.

'Today we need to discuss your options for moving forward. What do you plan to do now? You would have been briefed before your Dreamscape started about our residential community called Day Dream Waters. An estate of sorts for people like yourself who have returned. You are automatically offered tenancy as part of your package. You could have your own apartment; your neighbours would be people who understand what you've gone through,' John said.

'I don't even know what my options are. Do I have a job, a house? Money?' I asked, wiping my nose with the scratchy tissue.

'It's normal to have pockets and gaps in your memory for a while. Generally it's only temporary. According to your file, I see you have no immediate family alive, no significant other. You sold your house, and used the money to fund your

Dreamscape,' John said, scrolling through his iPad, reading notes on my case.

'So, I'm broke?'

'Actually, no. While you were asleep, an insurance claim came through from your car accident. You have a significant amount of money here.'

'Enough to go back into my Dreamscape, indefinitely?' I asked, suddenly feeling hopeful.

'Yes, it is.'

'Would I remember any of this? Would I remember Troy being gone?'

'Not if you didn't want to. You could literally pick up where you left off. There is always the risk that we may have to bring you out early, as you know from last time, should the project be terminated for some reason out of our control.'

'You mean like the government intervenes or something?' I asked. John nodded.

I had forgotten about that possibility. My heart ached to go back, to see Troy again, to live the life that had become normal for me. But now that I had experienced losing him for the second time, I wasn't sure I could put myself through that all over again – even if it was just a possibility.

'Is there no way to guarantee that I wouldn't wake up?' I asked.

'We could certainly include a D-N-W clause in your new contract.'

I frowned in confusion.

'Do Not Wake,' he explained.

I thought on that for a moment. 'Would that be like a kill switch?'

'Exactly.'

I thought back to my final moments with Troy, hugging him at the airport. It had all felt so real. His last words to me, 'live your life for you now'. I had lived so long for him – to see him grow and flourish, to experience all the opportunities that were taken from him. I didn't even know what living a life for myself meant. The only thing I was sure about was Troy, and what he would want me to do.

'If I'm dead, my memories – real or imagined – are gone too. I'm not ready to let them go just yet. And Troy wouldn't want me living in a dream.' I took a deep breath as butterflies filled my stomach. 'Tell me more about this Dream Day Waters place.'

Elephant and Wheelbarrow

Linda Kemp

'Belle? She's a nutjob,' Matty says, sipping his beer. 'You should stay away, that's my advice.'

It's Friday night. We're at the pub on Bourke Street. I asked him about her five minutes ago and he launched into a tirade about her instability, all the ways she screwed over Matty's brother's best mate, Leo. I'm sorry I asked.

'You don't think your point of view is coloured by Leo?' I ask Matty.

'Come on,' he responds. 'She really screwed him over.'

Typical Matty. He's got it arse-backwards.

Belle whirled into my orbit two years back. A group of us got together to farewell Matty's brother,

Henry, who was off to backpack around Europe for six months. Leo arrived late with Belle, his new girlfriend. They were flushed and breathless. Her cheeks were pink; her eyes sparkled like the sequined top she wore. Matty and Leo pumped hands and Leo murmured something that caused Matty to roar as Belle blushed. She bowed her head, looked downwards. Leo was a dickhead. I never understood what Matty and Henry saw in him.

'Hey,' I said, when she stood next to me at the bar. 'What're you drinking?'

She turned to face me. 'Have we met?'

'Ollie Morton. Matty's friend.'

'Belle Robinson. With Leo.' She nudged her head in his direction.

'Can I buy you a drink?'

'Aperol Spritz, please,' she said to the barman.

I tossed my credit card on the bar. 'I got it.'

'And five James Squires.'

Fuck. I was committed now.

'Gotchya.' She winked at me. 'This band, hey? Whaddya reckon?'

The barman tapped my card as she called for Leo and his crew.

'Thanks. Owe you one.' She laughed, sending a buzz up and down my spine.

If she weren't Leo's girlfriend, I would have made a move then. I watched her walk away; her top was backless, showing those pointy bones at the shoulders and her narrow waist. I couldn't drag my eyes away as her hips swayed sensuously left to right. Left to right.

Eight months ago, Belle and Leo broke up. Leo was acrimonious; spewed blame at Belle's feet like a drunken sailor, while she remained silent. Lips sealed in an act that, to me, looked gracious, given all she'd been through with him. Now, I figure enough time's gone by for me to ask her on a date.

I stare at my beer glass. 'So Leo won't mind? He won't think I'm cutting his grass?' I ask Matty. I'm not sure why I care.

'Nah, mate. He's done with Belle. She's a bitch.'

As soon as Matty and I are done here, I'm calling her.

'How's all your shit?' I ask. Matty's getting married in five months and I guess I should seem interested, at least for a while.

'Oh Jesus, man, it's intense. Marzia's reaching fever pitch with the invitations. The supplier's just not to be trusted, you know?' He mimics her accent, rolls his eyes.

As he finishes his beer, I realise I feel sorry for Marzia. Matty can be an arsehole sometimes. If they get through this stage, though, I think they could be solid.

'On that note, I gotta go. She's got me on a short leash.' Matty slaps my back as a farewell.

'Check ya. Thanks for the beer,' I say, pulling my phone out of my suit pocket. I scroll through my contacts. She's there, not under B for Belle, but saved as PYT, a nod to the band in the pub the night we met. A hideous five-piece doing Michael Jackson covers. Off key, off rhythm, but persistently upbeat.

'You never answered my question,' Belle said, later that night on the dance floor. She was bouncing about with a girlfriend; her tits jiggled under her top.

'What question?' I asked, drunkenly dancing with a nameless one hanging off me. I pulled her closer to me. She felt the hardness from my boner and glanced up, beaming widely.

'The band. Whaddya reckon?' They were doing a crap job of *Pretty Young Thing*.

'Total shit. You?'

'Same,' she yelled.

The nameless one glared at her: back off bitch! She pulled me away from Belle, drew her arms around my waist and ground her hips into my groin in the time-honoured cue of 'let's fuck'.

Three days later, at Tullamarine, when we all gathered to see off Henry, I saw Belle standing apart from the group, texting, her fingers madly tapping at the screen. I checked around for Leo. He was in a huddle with Henry and the guys. Heads down, laughing. Pulled by a magnetic force, I made my way to Belle.

'Hey,' I said.

She looked up, smiled. 'Oh. Hi. Ollie, right?'

'Yep.'

She continued to tap on her phone. 'Sorry.' She looked up again, shrugged. 'Work.'

'Right.' I felt like a teenager. Uncertain, unable to walk away, but feeling like I should give her space.

'That's done.' She glanced around. 'Sorry,' she repeated. 'Just had to check in with my boss.'

'Right,' I said again, cursing myself for sounding lame. 'What is it that you do?'

'Media/comms manager with a foundation.'

'Oh, great.' My voice sounded clunky; the words hit the floor like wooden blocks. 'Which one?'

'Balloons For Learning.' Her gaze lingered just beyond my right shoulder. 'Heard of it?'

I shook my head.

'Nah, not surprised. It's not well known.

The organisation didn't even have a comms strategy before I came on board. My job is to get us out there, build a profile in the wider community, get more donations.'

'What's their aim?'

She slid her phone into her back pocket. 'Helping at-risk students stay in school. Get the most out of education.' Her face lit up; the passion and purpose she found in her work danced in every syllable as she kept speaking, 'Education is the key to a better life. Some of these kids BFL helps are stuck in a poverty lifecycle. Their future's bleak. By creating programs, we can help them see learning is fun as well as meaningfu—.'

Her eyes clouded grey. 'Sorry, gotta go.'

And she was gone. I turned to see Leo's arm wind tightly around her waist. He held her close, like a trophy. Didn't let her go while Henry walked through customs. I inched my way to the back of our group when I heard Leo offering to buy a round of drinks. Left as soon as the sliding doors closed, couldn't bear to see Belle with Leo. Her face concrete: hard, dull, ashen.

Matty's gone and I'm alone at the table in the pub. I press the green handset icon on my phone, listen, sweating, as it rings.

'Hello, Belle Robinson speaking.'

My heart races when I realise she must not have my number stored in her phone. What if she doesn't remember me?

'Belle, this is Ollie Morton. We met through Leo's mate, a few years back?'

She waits a beat; I hear something in the background. Papers shuffling maybe, or she's mouthing a conversation to someone. Abort the mission, my mind yells. I'm about to pull my phone from my ear.

'Ollie, of course I remember you. Michael Jackson cover band, right?' She laughs that spine-tingling chuckle. I feel it, electrifying, warming, enticing.

'That's right.' I breathe out. 'How are you?'

'Great, thanks.' She pauses. 'You know, I'm glad you called. I lost your number.'

'Yeah?' It's the only response I'm capable of making. Blood has rushed from my brain, rendering me incoherent. I'm lost in a visual of Belle and me together. Laughing, eating, talking, fucking. I cross my legs.

'Do you wanna grab a drink sometime?' Her voice wavers.

'I'd love to.' Fuck it. Go for it, Ollie. 'I'm at the pub now, actually. Just had a drink with Matty. Do you wanna meet right away?' I check my watch. It's 9 pm.

'Sure can. Which pub?'

'Elephant and Wheelbarrow.'

'Oh great, I'm still in the city. I'll be there in twenty.'

My phone slides out of my grasp as I hang up. I wipe my palms on my trousers.

Minutes pass like hours. When she arrives, I wave. She strides towards me; her dark brown hair falls in waves, licking her shoulders and face. She wears a white shirt and stovepipe suit pants, with heels so narrow and high I wonder how she walks.

'Ollie! It's good to see you! How are you?' she asks, planting a kiss on my cheek.

'Yeah, I'm alright. You?'

'Great now. I've had a shit week at work. So glad you called me.' She flicks a swirl of hair over her shoulder. I drink her in, from her feet to the undone button between her breasts, to her neck and chin, up to the crown of her head. Her lips are full like they've been stung by a bee. Pink and glossy. I guess it's lipstick or something.

'Why's that?'

'What? My shit week or that I'm glad you called?'

I only want to know the latter. But I answer, 'Both.'

'OK, work's boring, so I'll be quick. Boss is a micro-managing boomer. Can't stand her. Enough?'

I nod, even though I know there's more to her

work story. The foundation she works for is now one of the most well-known education charities in Melbourne. In those two years since our conversation at Tullamarine, she's lifted its profile substantially.

The corners of her lips curl upwards. It's a smile, but shy, nervous. 'I've always liked you Ollie. I felt a connection between us that first night. But you were with that girl. She was fierce.'

No words come.

'And I've wanted to ask you out for months, but I lost your number.' She draws breath. 'Actually,' she goes on, a dark shadow falls over her face. 'I didn't lose your number. I had to delete it. Leo checked my phone regularly to see who I was in contact with.'

'I see.' A rising anger and desire to punch Leo restricts my voice to a dry whine.

'Sorry, I know he's your friend, bu—'

I cut her off. 'He's no friend of mine. I only know him through Matty.'

'OK.'

'Leo's a dick,' I say. 'Anyway, what's your poison tonight? Aperol Spritz?'

She laughs and I feel the shiver again. 'Nah, I'll have a pinot noir, please.'

'Be right back.' My chair scrapes loudly over the wooden floorboards.

The barman's busy; he's making someone's cocktail. As I wait my turn, my mind rests on that sweltering January day when we all met up at the Espy. The third time I saw Belle, about four months after Henry's departure. She was holding onto Leo like he was her life raft, limping as if she were eighty, not thirty-something. Her floppy hat covered her face, and her long-sleeved blouse, her arms. I thought nothing of it.

'Looks like Belle's stepped outta line again,' Matty said to Marzia. I was standing next to them; he didn't lower his voice.

'You mean Leo's been a controlling bastard again?' asked Marzia.

'Marz,' Matty said. 'He's animated, that's all.'

'He's a violent prick. You ever try that shit on me and we're done,' Marzia threatened.

I looked at Belle again. This time with the scales peeled from my eyes. She was stooped, bent awkwardly in the middle. The hat over her face poorly hid a yellowing bruise on her cheek.

'Does he beat her?' I whispered to Marzia. I felt a burn in my throat. My fists opened and closed involuntarily by my side.

'Christ, Ollie. Catch up will you?' She walked away.

I breathed in slowly. I glowered at Leo. In vain.

He didn't notice me. Too busy frilling like a male peacock in front of his try-hard mates.

Belle was leaning against a wall, talking to Marzia. She was in tears. Marzia rubbed her shoulder, tenderly. I made my way to them.

'Ollie, our hero,' Marzia sarcastically whispered. 'What can I do for you?'

I ignored Marzia. Belle looked at me. Her left eye was still blood shot.

I gasped. 'Have you seen a doctor?' I realised my stupidity as soon as the words were uttered.

'Leo is a doctor, idiot.' This from Marzia. She cocked her head to one side, looked at me as if examining a specimen in a petri dish.

'Thanks Ollie,' Belle whispered. 'I'm fine. You should go. You'll only make things worse.'

I pay for the drinks and return to Belle.

'One pinot noir for you,' I say.

She puts her phone face down on the table. 'Cheers.' She sips, places the glass on the pub coaster. Her fingers are long; the nails coated with pink polish. I peek back to her lips. The colours match.

'You know, Belle,' I begin. 'I'm sorry I didn't do more to stop Leo from doi—'

This time she interrupts me. 'Nope. Don't say it.' She clears her throat. 'It's in the past. I've had a lot of counselling sessions.'

'Still though…'

'Enough,' she says softly, but with a force that makes me blink. 'Really. I don't want it raised again. Leo's a bad man. He's behind me now. I'm moving on to better things.'

Does she mean me? Did she agree to meet because she wants me, too? My thoughts tumble and I realise I know nothing. I drown again in the incomprehensible ocean of women's mating rituals.

She grabs her glass. She takes a sip. 'Tell me, what are you doing these days? Still an engineer?'

'Consultant now.' It's a big deal. I'm the youngest consultant the business has ever employed. I've worked my arse off, eyes on my end game: home ownership before thirty-five, personal super contributions. Future-focussed. Each step a carefully considered move on my career chessboard. But I tell her none of this. 'I'm with a big corporation that does PPPs.'

'I don't know what that means.'

'Public-Private Partnerships. We partner with government departments to look after publicly owned assets.'

She screws her nose up. 'Like the trams, trains?'

'Yeah. Roads and buildings, too.'

'Is it interesting?'

'Like any job, I guess. Some days are good, others boring as batshit.' I pick up my schooner, finish my beer. 'Keeps me busy.'

I ask about her job and she blocks me with a straight bat. 'Told you already. Nothing much else to say.'

'I know that can't be true. BFL is high-profile now.'

She shrugs. 'A footy player or two always helps. TV personalities, too.'

'Don't dumb it down, Belle. You've done great.' I pause to see if she'll respond. When she doesn't, I continue. 'You should feel proud of what you've done there.'

Staring downwards, as if she's curious about a speck in the floorboards, she whispers, 'Thanks.' Those pink-polished fingers grasp her wine glass. The silence between us is heavy, almost damp with anticipation and tension. Then, her voice as smooth and dark as treacle, she says, 'Seeing anyone?'

'Nope.' I can't meet her gaze. My hands hold onto my empty glass. I wish I hadn't finished my drink; it would give me something to do. I spin it around.

'Why'd you call me?' she asks.

'Belle.' My voice is raspy. I slowly raise my eyes to meet hers.

She moves her head close. 'Go on,' she taunts, her lips almost graze against my own.

My dick swells inside my suit pants. 'I wanted to see you.'

'Why? Because you felt guilty when you knew what Leo was doing to me?' Her words sound harsh, but her voice isn't. Her eyes are soft, kind.

'What? No!'

'Then why?' Her breath is warm, wine-scented.

'Do you want to finish this somewhere else?' I ask, emboldened by the conversation.

She downs the last of her wine. 'Where did you have in mind?'

I tell her my place is a fifteen minute tram ride away while I visualise the state I left it in this morning. She opens the Uber app on her phone. I'm going room-by-room in my mind's eye, and feel confident the place is good enough for female company. I place my hand over her own and say, 'It's 10.40 on a Friday night. The tram'll be quicker.'

She nods, slides her phone into her handbag, and we leave the pub. It's a balmy night; the inky black sky is a canopy above the city.

'OK. We need the 72, we can hop on at Swanston Street.' I sling my arm around her shoulder, and she curls into my shape like a comma. We stroll down Bourke Street towards Swanston. The city buildings stand as sentries; their lights a thousand tiny eyes watching us.

'It's beautiful isn't it?' Belle asks, gazing upwards, like she's had the same thoughts.

We run the last few metres to catch the tram that's pulling into the stop. No seats, so we stand, gripping onto the overhead strap hangers. Belle crashes into me when the tram abruptly stops. I hold her steady with my free arm. She lifts her face to mine. We grin at each other like lunatics.

Minutes later, I ding the bell for the tram to stop. It's dark, quiet when we disembark.

'Just down here,' I say, more to splinter the silence than a direction.

Our footsteps trudge on the road in unison. The sound throws my mind to the penultimate scene in *Fury* where over two hundred SS soldiers crunch over a gravel track towards the disabled US tank and its four inhabitants. I shake my head; loosen the correlation of the sound of Belle and me walking with the image of approaching doom. She's beside me, my dream woman is about to step into my home, into my reality. I don't want to screw this up, can't risk a random movie scene tanking my performance. Almost chuckle at my pun.

I glance at her; she's watching where she walks in the dark, unfamiliar street.

'Belle, I'm glad you found the strength to leave him.' It's a whisper, a small murmur that booms in the night.

She doesn't respond. An agonising moment in time where my mind oscillates between self-deprecating thoughts and wondering if she heard me.

Belle pulls on my hand. I turn to her. Her hand touches my cheek, and she kisses me. 'Is it very far to your house?'

I shake my head. 'Nope. It's this one.' I push the front gate open and walk to the door. She's behind me; her arms wrap around me and I feel her breasts press into my back. I stifle a moan and my fingers tremble as I unlock the wooden door. We step inside, her fingers interlocked at my waist, clutching me like she's my shell. It's then I realise, we are each other's home.

Love Looks Like

Laura Pettenuzzo

There are seven billion people in the world, and you will always be my favourite. It takes patience, now, to love you like we used to. There's no point prompting you about appointments or conversations. I cannot share details of my life with you and hear about yours in exchange.

Whenever I was lost, I would show up on your doorstep, and with your hugs and gentle affection, you would show me the way forward.

Love used to look like playing board games together, like sleepovers and junk food and jokes we'd share with no one else. Now, love looks like cleaning your shit from the floor and saving you the embarrassment of knowing about it.

I cannot stop this change or take your pain away. But I can show up. I can hold your hand and I can meet your smile with my own. I will love you long after your final breath; my protector, my angel, my Nonna.

Nonna forgets, as time takes its toll on her body and her mind, when she's seen us last. She forgets what she's eaten, if she's taken her medication, and the puzzles that we make together. I know there'll come a time when she reaches for my name and doesn't know it, but I refuse to believe that our love will ever be lost.

My family complains about her confusion. They mock her adherence to routine, the way she clings to consistency like a child.

'All she cares about now is when her lunch will arrive. And when it does, she stuffs her face,' says her daughter.

I hold my tongue, knowing that arguing is futile, that anger and cruelty are the manifestations of their grief.

The loss of her independence hits Nonna hard, and after we move her into the nursing home, I visit her at least once a week – more often if my schedule will allow it.

It is fitting, then, that as the person I've loved most in the world begins to leave it, I meet someone who might one day equal her in my affections.

Nonna and I have lunch together when I visit. I bring a sandwich or leftovers from the night before, heating them in the staff kitchen.

Stella is the first one I meet, and of all the carers who work with my grandmother, she quickly becomes my favourite.

I hear Stella's laugh before I see her, high and lilting, in harmony with my grandmother's hoarse chuckle. I tiptoe through the carpeted halls, trying not to wrinkle my nose at the inescapable, hospital-like scent.

Hovering in the doorway, I take in the scene. Nonna has had a haircut. The soft white fluff on her head has a shape now, and she pats it appreciatively before turning her attention to the woman behind her.

'Shall I push you in?' The woman asks, her hands already poised on the back of Nonna's chair.

Nonna nods, and I watch the young woman at work. She is gentle with my grandmother, and this is what I notice first, what draws me to her.

She treats my Nonna as though she is the most important person in the world, as though she recognizes that this frail old lady is the most important person in my world.

'Can I help you with the cutlery?' this marvelous human asks, and Nonna shakes her head. This, at least, she will do herself. I grin, seeing my own stubborn streak reflected in her.

Nonna catches sight of me. 'Bella mia – I was wondering when you would come! Sit down – do you have some lunch?'

I sit, and when I pull out my lunch, Nonna nods approvingly. 'Now I happy,' she says, 'when I see you eat.' To the woman who is now filling our glasses with water, Nonna adds, 'This is Celeste, my granddaughter. She is very kind, very smart. She is at university and she do very well.'

If I had the right complexion for it, I'd be blushing. 'Nonna, I'm not—'

The young woman laughs. 'Celeste, I've heard a lot about you. You're studying psychology, and you're a painter, right?'

I nod, and she continues. 'I feel like I know you already! Audrey tells everyone about you. It seems like you two share a really special bond. Not many of the residents are visited by their grandchildren, let alone weekly. Anyway – what am I saying? It must be weird for you that I know so much about you. I'm Stella, and I'll be one of the personal care attendants working with Audrey.'

I shake the hand she offers me, strangely reluctant to let go.

Stella leaves us to attend to the other residents in the dining area, but she checks in with us regularly, making sure that Nonna has enough cushions supporting her back, that there's nothing more she can offer us.

Nonna and I eat mostly in silence, although she tells me several times about the succulent I brought her for Christmas, how it sits on her windowsill where it will get the most light, and how she waters it every day with the watering can she brought with her on the boat from Italy. 'That watering can,' she says, 'is older than your mother!'

'Wow!' I say each time, as if it is new information. I've read every article I can find about cognitive decline, and they all say that it's best to go along with these moments of repetition. Reminding Nonna of things she's forgotten will only cause her distress.

All the while, I keep an eye on Stella. She's the youngest of the care attendants by at least a decade, and the others act as though their age confers superiority and authority. Instead of biting back when they criticise her methods of feeding the residents, she gives her colleagues a gracious smile.

Her keys dangle from a lanyard on her neck,

and next to them are two key rings: Van Gogh's sunflowers and a miniature Simba.

This girl is a fan of art and the Lion King and – most importantly – my Nonna. She's perfect.

But could love really bloom here – could I allow it?

I notice the badges on her shirt the same day my mother does. The rainbow on her collar, next to the plain 'she/her' bring a smile to my face, and a disgusted frown to my mother's.

The door has barely closed behind Stella when my mother's dissection begins. She leans forward in her seat, relishing the opportunity to pass judgement.

'Did you see those badges she was wearing? Do you think she's one of them? Not that I care, but keep it to yourself! And what's with the "she/her"? We can tell she's a girl!'

I take a deep breath, twirling my hair into tight ringlets. 'The badges are to demonstrate inclusivity for trans and non-binary people. I wear mine at work too. I have it in my handbag, actually.' I pull it out and place it on my collar.

My mother's eyes follow my movements, but she says nothing. Perhaps she doesn't want to wake my grandmother, asleep on the bed between us.

'Forgot something,' Stella whispers, hurrying back into the room and taking the clipboard from the bedside table.

She notices my badge and we exchange a conspiratorial smile. We are united in that moment in a way that my mother could never understand.

A few weeks later, I'm finally able to make a visit alone. Nonna is sitting up in bed, knitting a purple scarf. There's a half-eaten plate of vegetables in front of her. She sees me glance at her plate, and her eyes water.

'I no hungry anymore,' she tells me, wiping her eyes. 'I have no appetite – why?'

I shrug, unsure what to tell her. The answer, of course, is that her body has had enough. Her heart beats too slowly, kept in rhythm only with the aid of a pacemaker. Her skin is paper thin and patterned with purple bruises. Life is leaving her in increments, and I don't want to see it. I fill her room with cheerful chatter, as if the sheer force of my will can keep her here.

'I have some photos to show you,' I say, dropping my handbag and pulling out my phone. My grandma leans forward, pushing the plate aside.

We flick through images of my pets and the books I'm reading, anything I've seen during the week that I think she might enjoy. She cannot see the rest of the world, but I can bring it to her. I can be her bridge, just as she has always been my compass.

After a few moments of silence, Nonna speaks. 'Is Stella working today? She is nice. She is my favourite.'

'What?' I gasp, feigning indignation. 'I thought I was your favourite.'

My grandmother pauses in her knitting to catch my gaze. 'You are, bella mia.' She squeezes my hand to emphasise her point. 'She is my favourite from here.'

'Well, then,' I say, mollified. 'I suppose I can allow that. I agree, actually.'

A week later, I bring several balls of wool from Spotlight, only to find that the unfinished scarf has been discarded in the wardrobe.

When I take it out, Nonna looks at me blankly, so I try a different tack, pointing to a book on the table. 'What are you reading?'

Nonna tries to stand, her gnarled fingers gripping the table for balance, reaching for the book.

'I'll get it,' I tell her. It's *The Alchemist*, and when I show it to her, she wears the same blank expression she'd given the wool.

'Is that yours?'

'No,' I say, feeling the reality of her decline like a kick in the stomach. Blinking back tears, I add, 'It was here when I arrived. I thought it was yours.'

I sit in one of the chairs just as Stella rushes in, blonde hair disheveled.

'Hello, Audrey. I think I left—' she breaks off and blushes as she spots me, the book still in my hand. 'I was reading that during my lunch break yesterday. Sorry, I must've forgotten—'

'No worries.' I hand her the book. 'It's a powerful read.'

'I reread it every year! We should discuss it over coffee sometime.' She clutches it to her chest and notices my teary eyes. 'Gosh, Celeste, are you okay?'

I try to tell her that I'm fine, but the words are stuck in my throat. 'Not – not really.' I glance at Nonna, who has closed her eyes, apparently asleep. 'She's getting worse every time I visit.'

'That sucks.'

There's no sugar-coating with Stella. I don't have to hide my hurt, don't have to concede that my loss pales in comparison to that of my family. I'm safe with her.

A week later, we move Nonna to the High Dependence Unit. I bump into Stella as I'm packing up Nonna's belongings.

She steps into the room, closing the door behind her. 'I'm so sorry your Nonna is deteriorating so fast. They'll be able to give her a greater level of care on the Dahlia Ward. But—I'll miss you.'

'Thanks.'

She turns to walk away, but I cannot let it end like this.

'Hey, Stella!'

She turns back, and I muster all my courage. 'How about tomorrow – for that coffee?'

Stella beams. Her smile is a sunbeam and I am glowing beneath its warmth. 'It's a date!'

You are my true north. Your affection has been a light through every patch of darkness, and you have brought Stella to me, a different kind of light.

This is what love looks like now:

Those moments, rare and precious, when you really see me, when you say my name and mean it.

Two girls who were friends first, and then

something more. A girl with stars in her name and goodness in her heart. And me, ready to let her in.

Body Bags

Mark Phillips

It's the sound of the birds I miss the most. I still remember them from when I was younger, whistling and chirping to each other from their homes in the trees, a symphony at the start of each day. I don't know when I first noticed the absence of sound, but I guess the birds' little lungs just couldn't cope with the smoke-filled air any longer and that was it. Or maybe it was the heat that killed them? No one ever talks about it.

So it's in silence that I walk to work. Even though the sun is little more than a blurry orange ball barely visible in the haze, I can already feel it heating up and I just know we're going to get hammered today.

I can smell the smoke through my mask – a scent it's never possible to truly escape, embedded into clothes, onto skin, into hair, no matter how many times you wash and scrub. At night, the baby wakes crying and coughing and gasping for fresh air, and Laura and I lie in bed straining our ears until we hear the steady sound of his wheezy breathing again, and we can relax until the next time it happens.

I find Viktor sitting in the small porta cabin that passes as an office and a tearoom at the depot, sipping a cup of instant coffee and going through the list of jobs he's been sent from head office. The dark marks around his eyes tell me he didn't sleep much last night either.

'You seen the forecast?' he says, barely looking up when I come through the door. 'Forty-eight degrees. Hope you're ready for a busy one.'

Leaning over him to scan the list on the computer screen, I see there's a dozen jobs there already. Last night's casualty rate was particularly high.

The sound of the radio drifts from the bench, a newsreader running through the morning headlines in between advertising jingles and classic rock hits: new bushfires out of control in the north-west; hundreds of dead fish as an algal bloom chokes a river; forecasts of more economic pain as the drought enters its third year; more blackouts interstate; and speculation that the government will have to impose further water restrictions as dam levels hit single figures.

Viktor throws the dregs from his cup into the kitchen sink, then stands at the window in silence, looking out into the brown murk, thick as a winter fog even though the fires are hundreds of miles away.

'How many days is it since we last had rain?' he asks, still staring out the window.

I glance at the calendar on the wall. 'One hundred and fifty-three.'

'You'd think there was nothing left to burn.' He turns away from the window. 'Well, that list's not going to get any shorter with us standing around chin-wagging,' he says. We pull on our protective gear and wearily he tosses me the keys.

Viktor places a few two-litre bottles of water in the gap between our seats. 'Keep your hydration up. I don't want to have to carry you away in a body bag.'

It's still early and there's no one else on the road apart from a few tradies darting here and there and the occasional lumbering commuter bus, its lights spearing through the dust and smoke haze before it emerges into full view.

Even though the windows in our truck are fully closed, we wear our masks and don't talk on our way to the first job. Maria Zanetti. Seventy-four-years-old, died overnight.

There's no movement in the quiet cul-de-sac, but I can feel eyes on us from behind the curtains of every house. When one of our trucks with the big BRADES logo is in the neighbourhood, it can only be bad news, and the local gossips will be checking to see which house we pull up in front of. I back into the driveway of a non-descript orange brick home and wait by the open tailgate while Viktor goes to the door.

Eventually a balding middle-aged man in a rumpled T-shirt and shorts appears. Tiredness is etched across his face, and his eyes are red-rimmed. Viktor flashes his identity card, shows him the documentation, and reads out the legal authority in a flat monotone. The man blinks rapidly, nods, then stands aside to let us in.

'She's through here,' he says, taking us down a dark, narrow hallway and past the kitchen, where I glimpse a middle-aged woman standing with her hand resting on the shoulder of an elderly man, until we arrive at a closed bedroom door.

With the curtains closed, it takes a moment for our eyes to adjust and see the old lady lying on the bed. She looks peaceful, almost serene. They've dressed her in her Sunday best – a bit of a waste in my opinion, given where she's heading – and it looks like they might have even put a bit of makeup on her face. I'm reminded of my grandmother in her open casket in the church when I was eight or nine, the first dead body I ever saw.

The heat in the room is suffocating. Later in the day, the air-conditioning will be shut off to save power for essential services, the solar panels on the roofs of most buildings rendered useless by the constant blanket of smoke, and once that happens, the corpse would rapidly decompose, its smell beginning to seep into every corner of the house.

Viktor and I work quickly, and in silence, while the man who showed us in watches from a corner. I wheel the trolley parallel to the bed, and on the count of three, we lift her in a single movement into the bag and zip her up. She's light and I could easily have hoisted her on my own, but it shows a bit more respect for the two of us to do it.

I begin pushing the trolley back up the hall, but I'm forced to stop when the old man I saw earlier bursts from the kitchen and blocks my way.

'You bastards!' he screeches, his knuckles white as he grips the side of the trolley. 'You fucking bastards! What gives you the right?'

I lift my eyebrows to Viktor. I'm still new to the job and he's in charge, after all. 'I'll handle this,' he mutters, removing his mask and moving towards the old guy with his hands up in the air in a conciliatory manner.

But there's no need. The woman who was in the kitchen grabs the old bugger and pulls him out of the way. He slumps, the fight gone from his eyes and offers no resistance.

'Dad, it's the law now,' she says. 'They're just doing their job.'

He collapses into her arms, his body shaking with gasping sobs. Viktor gestures at me to wait.

'Would you like to say goodbye one last time, sir?' he says gently. The old bloke looks up and nods mutely. I unzip the top part of the bag so he can see his wife's face and he shuffles over so he's standing right above her. He gazes down for a few seconds, saying nothing, then bends over and plants a kiss on her forehead. He turns away, and I zip up the bag and roll the trolley out to the truck.

'Sorry about that,' the middle-aged man says to Viktor as I slam the big doors shut at the back of the truck.

'Perfectly fine, sir,' Viktor says. 'It's just part of the job. We're used to people being a bit emotional during the collection.'

Viktor turns to climb into the passenger seat, but before he can heave himself up the step, the man is tugging at his shirtsleeve. He leans towards Viktor's face and I have to concentrate to hear what he is saying.

'What about the bounty?' the man murmurs, his voice just above a whisper. 'How much will it be? When will we get it?'

Viktor pulls his shirt away and looks down at him with disgust.

'That's your wife's mother in the back of the truck. Show a bit of respect.'

He slams the door shut in the man's face, and exhales deeply. I start the engine and we chug off down the street.

By lunchtime, we've picked up seven bodies – two from heat stroke, two from dehydration and three from respiratory problems – and the mercury is pushing 50 degrees. The refrigerator in the back of the truck is working overtime, and Viktor decides we should dump what we've got at the plant before continuing our run.

It's refreshing here in the refrigerator, unloading our cargo. I'd like to stay here for a while, but I'm conscious of the feeling of death all around me.

We remove the bodies one by one and throw them onto a pile on a pallet in a warehouse full of forklifts going backwards and forwards. From here they will be removed from the bags and I don't like to think too much about what happens afterwards.

They say it's a bit like a giant compost bin where the bodies are rapidly broken down into methane which is then used to generate electricity. It's the ultimate form of renewable energy, I guess.

Some bright spark in the government came across the idea last decade, after the great three-year heatwave and endless bushfires which left tens of thousands dead, mainly the old and the unwell. The cemeteries were rapidly running out of space and with the government scrambling for ideas for renewable energy sources, someone put two-and-two together.

At first there was resistance to the program. No one wants to see a loved one taken away to be processed into fuel for the energy grid. But when the government introduced a paid bounty for each body correctly disposed through the official channels, opposition mostly dropped off.

Viktor and I are just small cogs in the machine, with thousands of workers like us, doing the same job all over the country, many of them working for our employer: Body Removal and Disposal Environmental Services, BRADES for short.

※

By mid-afternoon, the air-con is going full blast in the cab of the truck, but there's no escaping the heat coming through the windscreen. We hardly talk because of exhaustion and our backs and arms are aching from all the lifting, but we've still got one more pickup before we can call it a day. Derek Johnson, aged 67.

I pull up at a nursing home, a grey, single storey building. There are only a couple of vehicles baking in the car park, and it takes forever for someone to appear when we ring the bell at reception.

'Sorry mate, we're short staffed today,' says the guy who opens the door. His staff polo shirt is stained with sweat marks and his eyes dart around nervously while he waits for us to bring in our gear.

I begin to feel uncomfortable about this place the moment I stick my head in the door. It's dark and the air feels stale and heavy. The nurse, or that's what I assume he is, leads us down a narrow corridor that reeks of boiled vegetables, and past a dozen or so closed doors, but we neither see nor hear any other signs of life.

He unlocks a door, and on the bed is a man who looks about 70, lying on his back in a pair of boxer shorts and a filthy singlet that must have once been white. The room stinks of piss and sickness, and there has been no effort to make the man look any more respectable for the last journey he'll ever make.

'No relatives?' Viktor asks, looking up from the notes he's been sent from head office.

The nurse shakes his head. 'So that means the bounty comes to the nursing home, right?'

We're in no mood to linger. Viktor quickly completes the paperwork, and after lifting the body onto the stretcher, we're out the door, glad to rid ourselves of the stifling atmosphere inside the building.

Loading the body into the truck, I have this lurching sensation in my stomach that makes me unzip the top the bag. I crouch over the body so no one can see and look closely at the face inside. Something's not right, and I lower my head until my right ear is just millimetres from the old man's mouth. Is the heat playing tricks on me? I'm sure I can feel a flutter of breath. I unzip him further and press my ear down over the man's chest. There's the faintest sound, a slow rhythm, but unmistakable.

'Viktor!' I whisper. 'I think he's still alive.'

Viktor hurries over and plunges two fingers onto the man's neck, feeling for a pulse. He holds still for half a minute or so and then looks at me in alarm. 'Leave it to me,' he says, pulling his phone from his trousers and punching the quick dial for head office. I hear him say his name before he walks away out of earshot.

While I'm waiting, I slam the back doors of the truck closed and find a spot in the shade, taking my drink bottle with me. On the other side of the car park, Viktor is pacing up and down with the phone to his ear, getting more and more agitated. Out of the corner of my eye, I sense movement in a window of the nursing home, a curtain being pulled open a crack and eyes peering out, but perhaps it's my imagination.

After a few minutes, he hangs up and curses loudly, then wanders over to me, shaking his head and furtively looking back to the reception of the nursing home.

'Head office says to just zip him up and bring him to the plant with the rest.' I can hear the reluctance in his voice. 'I've been ordered not to make a report or say anything. And you're to do the same. Understand?'

'But Viktor, he's alive!'

'Yeah, well he's hardly in the flush of good health, is he? Just do what you're told.'

Viktor's the boss and there's no point in arguing anymore. Plus, this place is giving me the creeps and I just want to get out of there.

'Look, I don't feel any more comfortable about this than you do,' Viktor says once we've driven off and put some distance between us and the nursing home. 'If it's any consolation, head office says the people back there — whoever they are — won't be getting any bounty payment.'

I've heard about these types of scams before, where someone will knock off an elderly person in their care for the bounty. But I've never actually witnessed one — or not knowingly.

It is almost four by the time we get to the plant for the drop off. As we climb out of the cab, Viktor warns me again not to say anything.

In the back of the truck, hidden out of sight, we both crouch over the body of the old man we collected from the nursing home. Gently, Viktor searches near his throat for the man's pulse, then shakes his head. In silence, we throw the body on the pallet with the others, just before a forklift arrives to take it away to composting bins.

On the drive back to the depot, we don't talk until we are inside the front gates. I park the truck but neither of us moves for a while, then slowly Viktor climbs out of the cab and I do likewise.

He sighs deeply. 'Look, I know what you're thinking. But that old bloke this afternoon… he was gonna die soon. If it wasn't today, it was tomorrow. You saw his room — no one's gonna miss him.'

I shrug and avoid his eyes.

'I don't like it any more than you do – but do I have to spell it out for you? If there's no more bodies, we're all out of a job. The whole bloody system would collapse.'

He takes a deep breath. 'Look, I was like you once but you've got to harden up. We can't save everyone. Just be glad you've got a steady job. Come to work, keep your head down and get paid. That's how I've survived for this long.'

When I still don't respond, his voice gets angrier.

'Just don't go getting any silly ideas, okay? Remember – you're still on probation, and there's hundreds of others who'd take your job in the blink of an eye.'

'Okay, okay,' I say. 'I get it: don't rock the boat. I'm not going to do anything stupid.'

Viktor seems to relent a little and his body slumps in exhaustion. He watches me closely, waiting to hear what I've got to say next and we stand there awkwardly in silence for what feels like hours before I clear my throat.

'Well, I'd better head home. Laura will be waiting for me.'

While we've been talking, a light breeze has begun blowing through the depot, providing no relief from the sweltering heat but strong enough to sweep away the smoke haze so that a few rays of sunlight can cut through for the first time all day.

I leave Viktor there, at the gate of the depot, and walk down the road in the searing heat trailed by my long shadow. My shirt is sticking to my back, the sun bearing down, and it all feels like a curse.

Fire Trap

Melanie Hutchinson

The searing heat blasted Kim as she stepped out onto the front verandah of her ninety-year-old sandstone bungalow that she'd inherited from her grandparents when they retired and moved closer to town. Hesitating for the briefest of moments, she hugged her four-month-old, Finn, tight to her chest and ran to her white Range Rover. The yellow front door heralded a sense of finality as it slammed shut behind her. The thick smoke from the surrounding bushfires roasted Kim like a piece of wet clay in a kiln, singeing the hairs on her arm. Trying not to breathe in the ash-filled air, Kim hurried to strap her baby into his car-capsule. Her fingers were like moist strands of spaghetti. Fumbling and slipping as she wrestled with the safety harness.

Angry plumes of smoke and ash smothered Kim as she hurried. Her eyes watered. Blinking, she could barely see as smoky fibres wrapped around her face. Gossamer thin tendrils made their way through her airways, prompting Kim to adjust the yellow silk scarf around her nose and mouth as she resisted the urge to cough.

The blackened horizon was now glowing red. Trespassing even closer since she last looked fifteen minutes ago. The smell of charred eucalyptus mixed with singed animal fur made Kim's stomach churn.

Baby secured, she ran to the driver's side and clambered in just as her mobile rang. It was Tony. Kim turned on the engine, shoved her seatbelt into its holster and pushed the answer button. It was sweltering inside the car. Sweat ran down her neck and back. She cranked the air-conditioning as cold as it would go.

'Kim, where are you? Have you left?' his voice projected a little too loudly.

'We're leaving now,' Kim rasped.

'You mean you haven't left yet? For God's sake, Kim,' Tony's voice cracked as he spoke. 'I know some people have chosen to stay, but you should be out of there now. What are you waiting for?'

'Tony ... Not now ... We're leaving.'

Tony took a breath. 'Listen, you won't be able to get to the highway by the usual route. Those roads are closed. You've been listening to the radio, right?

'Yes T—' With phone squeezed between her raised shoulder and cheek, Kim put the car into drive and flattened her right foot to the floor. 'Where are you?'

'Bega. Your mum wanted to check in on Frank and Edie on the way. They're getting groceries. Not sure when we'll be heading to Tathra.'

Kim kept her eye on the horizon. The red glow intensified.

It was a menagerie in her car. Kim had squeezed in as many of their animals as she sensibly could: the two ducks and the drake in a cage, the only chicken she could catch and her five chicks in another cage, their two cats and dog. She thought briefly of her horses. The lump in her throat hadn't left since she opened the stable door and watched them bolt. The stench in the car – a mix of smoke, sweat and fear – spurred Kim on.

She stole a glance in the rear-view mirror. Finn hadn't stirred. *Can check on him later.*

'Gotta go Ton. I love you. I'll call … Bye.'

'Kim … You too. And the muffin.'

Killing the call as her tyres spun wildly on dry red earth, Kim careened down their long, dusty driveway. Smoky-red dust trailed in her wake. Her white Range Rover reflected threatening shades of red and orange.

Pausing at the end of the driveway, Kim eyed the horizon critically. Red dust swept past her car window. Squinting, she shivered despite the sweltering heat. The fiery glow had intensified. The thick darkened mass on the horizon rolled one way, then another, then towards her, then away. Kim studied this for a few more seconds ... then it seemed like waves of ash were crashing towards her.

Fifteen minutes. Maybe twenty, tops.
Think.

Kim's thoughts drifted to one of the many times they visited Granddad Frank and Grandma Edie on the farm. One of those lazy, early autumn evenings when the daylight lingered and the weather was still warm enough to wear a tee shirt.

Seated on their huge verandah in white wicker chairs pristinely preserved by Grandma Edie, Granddad had been in one of his storytelling moods. Drinking a cold one while Edie watched the cricket on their tiny portable telly, he told her about his narrow escape from a bushfire not long after he and Grandma Edie had moved to the farm.

Flattening her right foot to the floor once again, Kim pulled out onto the highway. Kim glanced at the pudgy bundle that was her baby strapped in his car seat. Somehow, he was still sleeping while the chicken squawked and nervously flapped about in the cage. *Please Finn, just keep sleeping. Please ...*

'We were out 'n about checkin' the paddocks,' Granddad had started. 'Been listening to the radio all mornin'. Reports said the fire was headed in the other direction. So I wasn't fussed. But it was on our way back. When we were around thirty clicks from the farmhouse. That's when we saw it: the devilish glow of hell on the horizon.

'So I stopped drivin' and watched it. Starin' at it for a few minutes, counting the seconds and staring. Little Jackie was starin' too. Although he was too much of a youngster to really know the danger we were in.'

Kim gritted her teeth as if that could somehow shake the story out of her head and concentrated on the road. The winds roared. More smoke and ash washed over the highway in billowing waves.

'Sure enough, it was headin' our way and it was gonna be on us in no time. I knew full well we'd never outrun it. Just reckoned we had to get to Barry and Bev's farm over the next ridge. Theirs was the only reservoir still with water in it. It was a long shot but we had no other option. I wasn't about to become chargrilled steak for that bloody monster.

'I floored it to their reservoir. I could see, lookin' in the rear-view mirror the fiery inferno getting ready to swallow us whole. I told Jack to undo his seatbelt and to jump when I gave the word. Then I drove the ute straight into the water and yelled at Jack to jump. Then I jumped too.

'Later we had a helluva time getting it out. Anyway, Jackie and I sheltered behind the ute's half-drowned nose and waited.

'I told Jack, *"When that monster comes over us, you just hold your breath and go under alright? No questions. Just do it. Don't come up till I tell you, alright?"* Jack was too terrified to answer. His little face just nodded. Sure as eggs, a few hellraisin' minutes later that monster raged right over us.

'When we came up for air after, neither your uncle Jackie nor your ol' Granddad had any hair on the tops of their heads! Your Grandma Edie was mighty pissed at me, with Jackie's blonde curls burnt off like that.'

A loud crack snapped Kim back to the present. Out of nowhere, an enormous, dried-out gum tree crashed down onto the road in front of her. Kim hit the brakes. Her overheated tyres skidded and squealed on the heat-buckled bitumen as she fought to keep control and avoid a collision with the obstacle that was now blocking her escape.

It's getting closer.

The blazing horizon was alive. Pulsing with fury. It ripped through the dry, drought-affected paddocks like a flaming reaper. It was moving faster than she had predicted. Kim knew they would never get out in time.

Time to test your story, Granddad ...

In a spur-of-the-moment decision, Kim did a U-turn and raced back down the highway towards her neighbour's property. Their reservoir still had water. She couldn't recall if they'd decided to stay and defend their property, and she didn't have time to drive down the long driveway to their farmhouse to find out. She sped down their gravel driveway until she spotted the body of water that she hoped would save them. Turning off the driveway into the paddock, Kim drove as fast as she dared, stopping her car just in front of the water. She climbed out and ran around to open the rear passenger door.

The terrified cats and dog leapt straight past her splashing into the water. She ripped the cage doors open – *sorry little ones, you're on your own* – and didn't even look at what the ducks and chickens did before her spaghetti fingers fumbled with Finn's car-seat harness until it opened.

Grief-singed fear silently wrapped itself around her, choking her. Yanking him out, Kim ran around the car and climbed into the driver's seat without closing the door. Clutching Finn tight, she hit the buttons to open the car's windows. As the glass simultaneously slid inside the car's four doors, Kim grimly drove into the reservoir as far as she dared.

She clambered out into the pungent smell of charred eucalyptus and animal flesh. Kim tried to stop her guts from dry-retching. *This monster must have us surrounded.* Holding Finn close to her chest she waded around the four-wheel drive to shelter in deeper water behind the nose of her car. They waited.

This better work Granddad.

Kim's mind raced as she considered how she was going to protect Finn from the fire without drowning him.

Heart pounding, Kim focused on her breathing and began counting the seconds, occasionally looking up to gauge where the thick darkened mass of ashen smoke was. She kept counting until four minutes had passed. Then six minutes. Ten minutes. Fifteen minutes. Sixteen minutes. Seventeen minutes. She wondered whether her neighbours, Bill and Maggie, had stayed. Their house was too far away to see.

It should be here by now.

Kim tentatively stood up and looked around. Finn started squirming in her arms. It had been hours since his last feed. She looked down at him. 'Shhhhh ... Shh ... It's ok Finn. It's ok,' she whispered into his ear, gently jiggling him up and down.

Pulling Finn's face close into her chest, Kim stared at the air visibly thick with smoke. The fire was nowhere to be seen.

Could the wind have changed direction?

With an uncanny sixth sense that babies seem to have, Finn started screaming. Like he knew the danger had passed. He was starving and needed his mum to know it was time to feed him. Holding Finn close, Kim waded to shore and surveyed the smoky landscape. The cats leapt out of the water but the ducks and the dog stayed, eyeing the horizon. Kim looked back at her car and absent-mindedly noticed the chicken and her chicks quietly huddled on the edge of the backseat. Cold water trickled down Kim's legs from her sodden shorts. She shivered despite the scorching heat.

'Oi, Kim!' A familiar voice cut into her consciousness. 'Kim!'

Kim turned to see her neighbour Bill getting out of his ute. 'Kim, are you alright? Jeez, how's the little fella?' He ran towards mother and baby and extended his hand. 'There, there,' he said at the screaming Finn. 'I was out checking the sprinklers on the roof when I saw ya car in the reservoir here. Come inside, we'll fix ya both up.' Bill motioned to Kim to follow him to his ute.

'Ya know, we've plenty of room in the driveway if you want to park there next time.'

Kim shot a look at Bill who smiled.

'It's alright love. We all just had a close shave. Maggie and I thought you'd left with Tony and the rest of 'em yesterday,' he said as they got into the ute. 'We had no idea you were still here with the young'un. What were ya thinking staying here all by yourself?' Bill shook his head as the ute approached his house. 'Fire went and changed direction. It's ripping right through to the coast though. Last we heard they're evacuating south of Bermagui. Dunno exactly where but still waitin' on the latest update.' At the house, Bill opened the front door and ushered Kim and her baby inside.

'Wait, where?' Kim whipped her head around to look at Bill. 'Tony … Tony's in Tathra.' She fumbled at the pockets of her wet and muddy shorts and pulled out her mobile phone. A black screen stared back at her. 'Damn.'

'It's alright love, use mine,' Bill offered her his Nokia 3310. Taking it, she was grateful for its solid and reliable simplicity.

For a minute Kim couldn't remember Tony's phone number. Her head was spinning. She took a few deep breaths, her frantic mind slowly calming down to allow the jumble of numbers in her head to form a coherent string connecting her to Tony.

'Hello?'

Kim exhaled at the sound of his voice. 'Ton … where are you?'

'Kim?'

'Yes. Ton, I'm calling on Bill's phone. Mine's dead. Where are you? Are you ok?' Kim sounded more panicked than she wanted.

'Bega. Never made it to Tathra,' his voice crackled. 'Reception here's terrible. Tathra's surrounded. No way we're going there now. Tell me you're somewhere safe?'

'We're at Bill and Maggie's. The wind changed. We're fine, but Ton … We're gonna need a tow truck.'

Distorted

Jamisyn Gleeson

I wake up.

I wake up and I can't breathe.

I try to inhale through my nose; one nostril is runny like eggs and the other is blocked like it's caved in. I try through my mouth; I choke on my own spit. I sit up, hunch over and cough and hack and spit into the crumpled wad of toilet paper that sits on my bedside table. It turns red, shockingly red, like paint.

I stare at the stains for seconds. I thought I only had a cold. I sit and slouch and will myself to breathe. I try through the nose, I try through the mouth.

I drag myself to the hospital, coughing and hacking and choking on my spit all the way there. My legs are stiff and stone-like but I force them to take me to the front desk. The receptionist asks me what my name is and after I give it to him – mumbling and faltering – he directs me to a squashy seat in the waiting room.

I sit and slouch and will myself to breathe. In front of me, a boy with flushed cheeks sits cross-legged on the carpet. He curls his grimy fingers around a golden spinning top and gasps when it falls from his grasp. It spins and spins and spins its way across the floor like a nervous planet.

I stare at the toy until a woman in a white coat emerges and beckons me to follow her into an examination room. She asks me why I'm not breathing properly. She asks me why my breath stumbles. She asks me why I breathe. I try through the nose, I try through the mouth. She takes me to get an x-ray, a film of grey and white and black, to examine my internal organs. I thought I only had a cold.

The x-ray looks like a portrait of shadows and I don't understand it at all but I know that it's a chart of my own lungs. I've never seen my lungs before. A part of me is in awe that I have them. The doctor points to the chart and utters the word 'pneumonia'. Her eyes are wide and a little concerned and now

I'm frightened. I'm frightened by her wide and concerned eyes. Her eyes concern me. There's a poster on the back wall of an old man clutching at his chest because he's dying of pneumonia. Am I going to die like him? I cough. I thought I only had a cold.

The doctor's pen bleeds on freshly printed paper as she fills out a prescription. Her spidery scrawl says I've got to take seven pills a day to get better. The pills are large and red – shockingly red – and I'm scared they'll get stuck in my throat when I swallow them. Then I really won't be able to breathe – through the nose or through the mouth. They pass through though, they slide down with water. They taste like chalk. I smack my lips together.

My doctor ushers me into a smaller room and introduces me to a nurse who speaks in a soft voice. She's here for my life, but not for me. You need to lie down? she asks. I decline. I'll look like a dead body – stiff and stone-like. She sticks a needle into my left arm. It stings and the room sways. I feel like I'm a little fish swimming in a too-large tank. You don't have to look, she says, but I do, and watch her coax my life, my red, shockingly red life, into a tube. If she keeps going, I'll look like a shell, drained of all my internal organs and fluids. This is scary, no? she asks while my blood spills into the tube. We all know how we are born, she continues, but we never know how we are going to die. She removes the needle from my arm. It stings and the room sways. I'm going to get you a sticky tape, she says, and hides the puncture-mark underneath a wad of cotton. When she's done, she looks up from my arm, caps the tube and shakes it so that my blood races up its clear walls.

When I get home, I close all the curtains and collapse on my bed. The covers are cold and I'm clammy. I stare at the walls. They move. I move with them. We move. Everything is distorted. I feel like I'm a little fish swimming in a too-large tank. A large fissure runs across the ceiling in a jagged line. If I lie here long enough, it might crumble, collapse and crush me underneath layers and layers of plaster. Then I really won't be able to breathe – through the nose or through the mouth.

A series of sticky strands string themselves across a corner of the ceiling. It's web, I realise, web dotted with tiny black bodies – flies. They look like shells, drained of all their internal organs and fluids.

The spider, poised at the top of its web, descends to one of the struggling flies. Its legs are needle-like and decisive. I know that it has eight eyes plastered to its head but I can't see them twinkling. I want to call out to the fly, to warn it, but it won't be able to hear me underneath the blanket of web that ensnares it. I watch the spider knit the fly into a sticky spool. It does this masterfully, spinning and spinning and spinning the tiny body with its pointy legs. Am I going to suffocate like these insects? I cough and hack and choke on my own spit.

I could lie here for days and nobody would know that I'm not resting. The elderly woman that I live with – the woman made of brittle bones – might knock on my door when my body starts to stink and walk away when I don't answer, thinking that I've left something to rot in my room. But I'll be the thing that's rotting.

The fly stops moving. I can't breathe. I cough and hack and spit out a wad of phlegm that's red, shockingly red, like paint. I never imagined I would expel my life out onto a crumpled sheet of toilet paper. I thought that Death would steer clear of me for a few decades longer, but now they tease my tiny body with their masterful, pointy legs. My lifeline has been stretched like web for twenty years and now it's collapsing like tired rope.

Who will order the flowers for my funeral? Who will lie me down into a dark coffin while the Earth keeps spinning and spinning and spinning? I feel like a shell, drained of all my internal organs and fluids. I feel like a dead body.

I know there's a spider in here with eight eyes plastered to its head but I can't see them twinkling.

I'm concerned by its concealed eyes. Its concealed eyes concern me. I'm afraid that its spindly legs might find their way underneath my bed covers, pierce the skin of my shins and spill the life out of me. I curl myself into a ball. I thought I only had a cold.

I could take my last breath right now, while the wind howls outside my window, while the rain patters steadily against its sill, while time keeps spinning and spinning and spinning. I lie here, stiff and stone-like, staring at the ceiling and at the long fissure that runs through it. If I lie here for long enough, it might crumble, collapse and crush me underneath layers and layers of plaster. Nobody knocks on my door. If I stop breathing now, I won't have to worry about who will arrange the flowers for my funeral.

I pull my bedcovers over my chin and close my eyes. The darkness is silky and smooth. It hooks its spindly fingers around the vertebrae of my spine and pulls me further into its embrace. I feel like I'm being taken someplace deep and silent. I can think better here. I think about nothingness. I think of nothing at all. I no longer need to inhale the worries of the spinning world and exhale my own fears back into it.

I am stagnant, static, stoic. I like it here. I like that I like it here. I fade.

I feel like I'm floating for hours before the hooks loosen their hold and my dreamscape turns bone-white, flooded with light.

I wake up.

I wake up and I can breathe.

I sit up, hunch over and swallow my red pills with a mouthful of cold water. They pass through. I don't cough or hack or spit my grey, white and black lungs out of my chest.

I pad across the room and pry apart the curtains. Their velvet skins feel soft but strange, somewhat static. I squint at the sight of the sunlight that spills into my room – it's gold, shockingly gold – and I bask in its rays and try to absorb all of its warmth. I open the window and a breeze drifts by. It chases my stale, sick breath out of the room and creates tangles in the series of sticky strands that are strung along the ceiling. I know there's a spider in here with eight eyes plastered to its head but I still can't see them twinkling. I open the window a little wider, just in case the creature feels like hooking its needle-like legs over the sill and catapulting itself back outdoors.

I squint at the sight of the sunlight on my skin. It catches the silver hairs on my forearm and makes them glint, tinsel-like, ethereal. A black body buzzes past my ear and hums around the room. Its opaque wings beat at the air and I watch its fat body spin and spin and spin around in manic circles.

I stand by the window and watch mirages of light shimmer across the earth and blades of grass dance in the wind. I let the air caress my hair and heat my cheeks. It feels warm and thick, like melted butter. I stand by the window and breathe.

In through my nose and out through my mouth.

Becoming Cat

Jessica L Wilkinson

My partner has noticed a feline quality in my behaviour. You might think I'm speaking in metaphors, but don't get me wrong. I'm a straight talker. Tidy tongue. Last night in bed, she laid her hand on my sweating forehead. *You're hot as hell*, she said, and I let her have a little nip on the pinky. It is easy to mistake irritation for playfulness in the bedroom.

I've been bitten by cats before, but that's not how this happened. It's been a lurking rebellion in my genes, roused by the next door neighbour's retirement pursuits. He has become something of a successfully irresponsible fisherman; the smell of his bountiful catch – fresh and saltwater – has moved through our house bi-weekly for the past six months, snaking through a gap in the window frame of my study and passing through the kitchen to hang for hours on end in the lounge where we dry our clothes. At first, this brought a twitching sensation to my nose, like an unrealised sneeze. The tiny hairs across my chest prickled and tensed. My nail-beds swelled and relaxed in quick succession as if I had jammed my fingers in the door and the blood was thumping through. It wasn't long before my body unravelled.

snapper, salmon, herring

stretch the neck up

All mysteries can be traced back to a collocation of circumstances – a collision of particles ripe for impact. Let me explain. I'm a Professor in Gender Studies at New Plains University. My specialty is twentieth-century drag performance, though I dabble in eco-queer and post-feminist children's literature. I have been internationally praised for my insights into the queer animated gaze and won the Butler Award – a sort of Nobel for gender theorists – two years running. In my spare time, I write short stories of a Kafka-esque flavour. My protagonist is always a twelve-year-old girl with gender dysmorphia. My partner wants to know why I don't spread my limbs, experiment with other characters. *Spread your limbs*, she says, over and over.

Not all change is instigated by the fanatical and excessive activities of one's neighbour. It can be equally triggered by ironic encouragement, warmed by the steady heat of an invisible forward momentum. It is partly a question of whether or not you are willing to ride the swerve.

spreading my limbs

eel, trout, perch

My partner passes me her cardigans to smell each morning and I shake my head. *It's fine*. She shakes her head in turn and tells me I need a nasal operation, as if that makes perfect sense. *What does he do with them all, anyway?* She huffs out the door. As her car rounds the corner out of sight, I like to roll in the fishy perfume trapped in the knit of her cashmere garments.

bream, whiting, flathead

a little twitching whisker…

Last week, my partner found a dead mouse on the rug and she let out a little scream, then teared up to see a trickle of blood through its fur. *What happened to it?* she said, nudging it with her shoe, appalled yet drawn to its grizzly demise. I looked up at her with my eyes wide and hopeful, but she didn't respond to my affection. She is confused by my odd communication. My vocal techniques have become subtle and nuanced, a fact of which I am very proud. And yet, she is worried that I am pulling away.

Of course, it won't be long before she discovers that I have not been to work for six weeks. I have neglected my classes and missed several important deadlines. She will soon reject my nuzzling as an adequate expression of desire, and will show signs that she thinks I am good for nothing. She will push me from her bed and take a new lover, but it is important that I don't blame her needs.

tuna, bonito, kingfish

scratching hard

Perhaps you assume that I will end up roaming the alleyways and stalking vermin with my pearl eyes, or that I will curl myself into warm corners with the afternoon sun in my fur. *Purring*. Perhaps I will. For now, I will spend my days pawing at books, the remnants of my slipping skin. Words falling away like so many dead rhythms.

The Enemy

Odette Des Forges

'The best weapon against an enemy is another enemy.'
– Friedrich Nietzsche

It started with tiny things, so faint an outsider wouldn't even notice: a sideways glance at that extra glass of merlot, dropping healthier food in the shopping trolley like missiles released from the belly of a fighter jet, and meditation class pamphlets left on the kitchen table at suggestive angles. It was me in the beginning – I knew that – but as the weeks careened into months, he jumped onboard. He was the one that instigated phase two of the campaign against each other.

We were in an outdoor beer garden in Fitzroy, with the light autumn sun shining through the bare branches. Our friend, Leo, scooched out of the bench seating and pointed at his boyfriend's near-empty glass and ours. 'Another one?' he said as he picked up the depleted jug from the middle of the table.

'Oh, go on,' I said. Everyone else nodded in agreement and Leo walked off, his brogued feet crunched away against the dried leaves. His boyfriend, Craig, excused himself as well, and as soon as his figure disappeared through the door, Dan turned to me. 'Do you think you should have another one?' he whispered, though why I didn't know; there was no one else there.

'Why not?' I said.

'You've already had two.'

His face was so earnest I wanted to poke him in the eye, just to see the expression whisked from him. Instead, I swallowed the remaining inch of my tepid beer; it no longer felt crisp and cool against my tongue and I realised I didn't really want another one, but I was already tipsy and logic had left early to attend another party. 'So, what? So have you.'

We stared at each other silently as snippets of conversation from other Sunday pub-goers drifted around us; for how long we stayed like that, I didn't know, but in the corner of my eye I caught sight of Leo's lime yellow T-shirt and I looked over and smiled as he walked towards us. Dan smiled too but it was forced and lacked its usual warmth. The fresh jug was filled to the brim and the golden liquid sloshed over the side in mini waves as Leo walked up to the table. He held it above my empty glass. 'Tash?'

A small, indiscernible pause. 'Fill her up, good sir.'

Dan sighed under his breath, so lightly only I could make it out.

'The supreme art of war is to subdue the enemy without fighting.'

– Sun Tzu

With those few disapproving words, Dan had sounded his battle cry and I armed myself, ready to engage. This was our cold war. My passive behaviour was replaced by an active approach, yet it was still subtle enough that I could get away with claiming a misunderstanding. Dan was America, I was Russia – two superpowers that didn't know how to lose.

I'd hear the fridge seal snap and I'd look over and say, 'There's a lot of sugar and chemicals in coke.' I'd try to phrase it in a way that implied I was merely stating a fact; it was not a personal attack. Dan stared at me, holding the cool can in his hand and then walked off, muttering about 'just trying to relax after work.' I knew I'd ruined his enjoyment of the beverage and this gave me a kick of satisfaction.

Another time Dan was lounging on the couch on a Saturday morning with our beagle, Nacho, his socked feet resting on the coffee table, the music doco he was watching blaring from the TV when I barged in and knocked his feet off with a kick.

'Come on, let's go for a bush walk. It's not good for you to spend the whole day on your backside. Active body, active mind.' I knew I sounded like one of those manic 80s aerobics instructors, but I smiled falsely through the cringe.

During the walk I could feel Dan's resentful eyes on my neck the whole time.

A few days later, he got his own back though. I returned from a hot yoga class to find him sitting at the kitchen table eating a steak with aggressive incisions. He glanced up at me, then his eyes flicked down to my yoga mat.

'You know there's such a thing as exercising too much,' he said, his knife poised in his hand, the blade pointed at me.

'What?' I walked over to the fridge and grabbed a bottle of cold water.

'Yes, I read about it. It's not good to over-exercise. At your age, you need to be careful.'

I laughed scornfully. 'My age! I'm 35, not 80.'

Dan shrugged and went back to attacking his steak. 'Hey, it's just what I read. Don't shoot the messenger.'

※

What Dan dished out, he'd get back threefold though, so when two days later I spotted Macca's wrappers rolling around on the passenger seat of his car, I plotted an ambush. I collected them and waited in our darkened living room for him to return from his walk with Nacho. I heard the door click and I clasped my first missile with wild anticipation. As soon as his silhouette materialised, I launched the attack:

'What's—,' a tightly rolled Big Mac wrapper soared through the air and hit him in the forehead, *boom!*

'This—,' a scrunched-up fry packet skyrocketed and landed on his shoulder, *wham!*

'About!' a mangled soft drink cup tumbled onto his chest, *whack!*

It was just light enough to see Dan's shocked and confused face; all my anger slipped away, and I burst into uncontrollable laughter.

It hadn't always been this way. When I first met Dan at 28 – Dan with the cool grey jeans, the handsome face and the warm laugh – I would've told you I couldn't imagine us raising our voices at each other, let alone pegging takeaway remnants. And for the first few years of our relationship this was true.

We were one of those blissfully easy-going couples that people wanted to be around – that people wanted to be. Whenever I felt mad or disappointed by Dan, I remember us in the beginning – staying up all night talking and touching, our body parts always having to be connected in some way, legs thrown over each other's or me laying back on Dan's chest – and I would melt.

We used to dance around Dan's bedroom in our underpants to Elton John's 'Bennie and the Jets'. We used to play chess in our swimmers in the courtyard of my inner-city apartment block. We used to picnic in the Botanical Gardens with only ourselves and a block of cheese for company.

We were free with our kindness, giving with our smiles, open with our forgiveness, but we were different people then. We were building sandcastles in the sky; Dan was the guy in the band, making a living working for Creative Victoria on the side, and

I was the artist, working as a website designer to make ends meet. Now we are simply the guy that works for Creative Victoria and the woman that makes websites.

What is human warfare but just this; an effort to make the laws of god and nature take sides with one party.'
— Henry David Thoreau

As the months rolled on, the jibes became more pointed, more obvious, all pretense of subtlety blown out the bus window by a handmade pipe bomb. We started irritating each other on purpose. Irritation is what spurred my first charge into enemy lines.

Dan was sitting on the couch in boxers and a faded Bowie T-shirt when I entered and perched on the end of the couch. Dan didn't even look up, instead he continued to scroll through his phone. Just seeing him sliding his finger along the phone screen, staring at it vacantly made my temples throb.

'Mum asked if we wanted to do dinner next Friday night?'

Dan's finger continued to worm upwards against the screen; his eyes remained fixed.

'Dan, did you hear me? Dinner with Mum next Friday?'

He lifted his head, but his eyes weren't focused and when he looked at me, his blank expression filled me with rage. 'Ground control to Major Tom!' I yelled and, even in my anger, thought myself pretty witty considering his T-shirt.

'What are you on about?' he asked with irritation and that was when my brain shifted into autopilot. I moved over to Dan with Viet Cong stealth, swiped his phone from his hold and yelled in his face, 'I hate this bloody phone!' Then I flung it at the wall, where it hit with a loud whack and tumbled to the ground, rolling over to display a smashed mirror screen; seven years bad luck for me.

I apologised for that one. I knew it was a bit much. I organised to get the screen fixed and Dan said it was fine, to forget about it, but I suspected it wasn't fine, that he hadn't forgotten anything. My suspicion was validated just over a week later.

Dan had made a brazier from an old barrel. One chilly winter night, Dan and I huddled around it, cradling mulled wine cups to our chests. An arctic breeze jostled the sprawling flames to and fro but they continued to blaze, the warmth touching my skin between cool gusts.

'Maybe I should get my guitar, play us a few tunes?' Dan said as he watched the sway of the flames.

'Sure, if you want to be the wanker with the guitar around the campfire.' I smiled and he looked at me and laughed that warm caramel laugh of his. I sipped my mulled wine; it was sweet on my tongue and warm down my throat.

He climbed up the stairs and I could hear cupboards creaking open, objects being dropped on the hardwood floor and Dan's footsteps back towards me.

'I can't find it. Have you seen it?' He asked from the top of the stairs. Realisation dawned. I'd lent it to my brother over a month ago.

'Sorry, I let Nathan borrow it. I should have let you know. I'll get it back this weekend.'

'Well, that doesn't help me now, does it?'

'No, I am sorry, but you never played it, so I didn't think you'd mind.'

'That's not really the point. It's not yours to give away.'

'I know that, okay. I'm sorry.' My tone was now dismissive, and a weariness descended.

'It's okay for you. It would be a different story if it were something of yours!' Dan's voice raised and I became hyper aware of the neighbours overhearing us.

'Keep it down. It's only a stupid guitar.'

Dan's eyes opened wide and his cheeks flamed

like the fire. 'Only a stupid guitar! If it's something of mine, it's stupid, isn't it?'

'Shh! Stop it, Dan,' I said, using my *inside* voice.

'Right,' he said and stormed off indoors. Moments later he returned with my yoga mat and marched down the stairs with it slung over his shoulder like a rifle.

'What are you doing?' I hissed. He ignored me and strode towards the fire, slamming the mat down on the flames. I jumped up and tried to rescue it, but Dan shielded me, his feet shuffled along, and his arms stretched out to block me at every angle. The stench of burning rubber floated through the air.

Some days, trying to remember who we were grew harder and harder.

'Wars are not paid for in wartime, the bill comes later.'
— Benjamin Franklin

Not long after the Battle of the Burnt Yoga Mat, Dan and I were in the kitchen – morning operations being conducted in silence. He was at the table eating a bowl of Crunchy Nut and I was at the coffee machine watching the inky liquid drip into my cup.

'I think we should see someone. A professional,' he said, breaking the silence. It was like sliding down the wall of a glacier. I couldn't reply. I didn't want confirmation that something was wrong; I was happy to embrace the ostrich and bury my head deeper, hoping that I might burrow through to the other side.

A chair scraped against the floor and Dan's arms snaked around my waist; he pressed his lips into the back of my neck. 'It's okay to seek help, Tash.' Hot tears fell down my cheeks and all I could do was nod.

After Dan waved the white flag, I felt silenced; too afraid to cause a scene in case he brought it up again, but as time ticked along, my fear of retribution filled me with uncontrollable rage and I was rearing to break the ceasefire.

'We must concentrate not merely on the negative expulsion of war but the positive affirmation of peace.'
– Martin Luther King, Jr

Days later I was sitting on the toilet, holding that smooth, white stick I'd held so many times before. I thought about Dan on his boys' trip this weekend and how he was probably eating complete crap and drinking his body weight in beer. Probably saying what an unreasonable tyrant I was, too.

Fury emanated through my skin like hot coals; I decided it wouldn't be crazy at all to take the scissors to all his favourite T-shirts, but just as I was about to pull up my pants and orchestrate a raid on Dan's wardrobe, an image appeared on the little view panel and I watched two beautifully straight pink lines form. I stared at them.

I'd dreamed of seeing these two lines. I'd whispered to the universe about their arrival. I'd blown on eyelashes envisioning their presence, and there they were. My anger evaporated and I was filled with a calm a year's worth of meditating was never able to achieve. Within seconds the peace turned to excitement and I cried and I whooped and I kicked the air in triumph, before I rushed through the house to find my phone. There was only one person who would understand how I felt.

Dan picked up after two rings. 'Hey, what's up?' he said. He knew I wouldn't usually call him when he was with his friends.

I swallowed, not sure how to phrase it, but then I laughed, realising it didn't matter.

'Dan, we have a decisive victory.'

With & Without

Justine Stella

She is eleven and she knows what she's doing is wrong. But she's going to do it anyway. She's the only one who can. Her sister is too young. Her mum promised, after all. She's just helping her mum keep her promise. By doing the wrong thing.

She waits until her mum is standing in front of the CD player in the brightly-lit kitchen. Her mum picks up a stack of CDs that don't have covers. Her hands are clumsy and she drops them. The CDs scatter across the kitchen floor and the overhead light catches the shiny sides.

Even at eleven she knows this dropped handful of CDs will take her mum a long time to pick up and organise. Now is her perfect chance.

She opens the fridge door, lifts the cardboard box and walks to the door that leads to their backyard. Once outside, she crouches down and flips the hard plastic button that lets the foul-smelling liquid pour into the dirt.

She returns the empty cardboard box to the fridge, knowing her mum will assume she drank it all. She will never know her daughter helped her keep her promise to stop soon.

She helps her mum gather the CDs before tucking herself into bed.

He is seventeen and he knows hoping for something can be – will be – disappointing, but he hopes anyway. He is always disappointed.

His mum refuses to make eye contact. She shuffles through her handbag and pulls out random items. She is upset that the envelope with their rent money is not there. She tells him that it was stolen at her work. She amends her words to include the possibility that she lost it. He wonders how many times they will have this exact conversation before she finds a new excuse.

He uses his older brother's hand-me-down BlackBerry to send the real estate agency the total rent amount for the month. She says she will pay him back. He hopes so; his savings are nearly empty.

He then opens the photo app on the phone.

He didn't believe his brother until now. Their mum is losing the money, just not in the way he thought. Now he knows. He looks at the most recent photo. He took it yesterday after sneaking into the pokies. He was only inside for a minute, just long enough to take the photo. The photo is slightly blurred, but he can see his mother sitting on a stool with her back curved, one hand cradled around a white envelope. Her other hand is feeding a $50 bill through the machine's slot. He wants to confront her, wants to show her the photo and demand she stop lying to him. But he never has the courage.

His mum rifles through her bag a few days later when their electricity bill is due, spluttering about the disappearing envelopes. A month later she says the same again when the rent is due. He hopes she stops losing it.

He is always disappointed.

They meet when they are twenty-two. She no longer feels guilt for doing the wrong things. He no longer hopes his mother will pay her share of the rent.

When she stays at his house for the first time, they only know a little bit about each other. She falls asleep with his arms curled around her and wakes at 4 am to a rustling sound by her head. Squinting, she sees a figure open the drawer of the bedside table and pull out a flat black square. A sliver of yellow flashes. As the figure turns towards the door, she realises who it is and shudders.

He waits for his mother to close the door before he whispers, 'I need to find a hiding spot so she stops doing that.'

She is silent for a while before she sits up and takes hold of his hand. 'This is not okay. This shouldn't be happening to you.'

He squeezes her hand like a child does when crossing a busy road.

She is eighteen and therefore deemed old enough. She knows she is doing the right thing, but she wishes she didn't have to do it. She wishes her grandmother could still help. She wishes her sister were the oldest. She wishes her aunties hadn't had kids so that they could help.

She is alone as she signs her name on the visitor log and allows the nurse to search her bag. She expects to enter the Family Visiting Room, the colourful room she has always visited her mum in. But she's an adult now. The nurse escorts her to the ward. It is white.

Wobbly women fill the hallways and wide-eyed men sit in grubby recliners. One of the women grabs her arm. She's shaking so hard she can't unhook the woman's fingers.

But then she looks at the woman and knows she can't shake her off. It's her mum.

They sit outside in a tiny courtyard and her mum fills the space with noise. She writes a list on her phone of the things her mum needs: clean trackies, coffee in a plastic container (not glass), and smokes. She will bring them in tomorrow.

This is her new role.

She is an adult now.

He is eighteen and he wonders if he will ever learn to predict his mum's behaviour. He wonders if he will ever stop hoping for change.

He fills out the deferring paperwork online and then checks his accounts. He closes his laptop.

He pulls his wallet from his pocket and thumbs through the plastic cards. He slides his Myki card out of its slot and flips it between his fingers. Its balance is currently -$9.54. He drops it, letting it land lightly on a pile of his uni textbooks. He wishes he hadn't bought those textbooks. Or the new programs for his laptop. If only he'd saved all that money to put towards the bills. Maybe he can sell them. He wishes his brother would be more responsible and hold down a job for more than a week.

When he leaves his dark bedroom he's ready for his mum's excuses, but he can't help hoping he will see that white envelope as she searches through her bag. Maybe she just missed it when searching at the real estate office?

She makes eye contact this time, and he realises she knows he will cover it, just like always.

Her car is broken into only months after they start seeing each other and she asks her mother for a lift. She hopes she can rely on her mother to get them home safely; she knows that her mother's been well for nearly a year.

He sits in the back seat and makes small talk with her mother. She is quiet, content to listen to them chat. Together they all agree to meet tomorrow to sort out what to do about the damage to the car. When her mother drops them off and waves, she smiles but he bites his lip.

She turns to him, her eyebrows raised like McDonalds' arches. 'What?'

'There were empty beer bottles under the seats. I just want you to be prepared.'

She leans into him and wonders how long until the next hospital admission.

She is nineteen and is expected to be fully competent at being an adult. She understands that she is not the worst off. She knows that everyone assumes she will make sacrifices. Maybe one day she will make sacrifices and feel good about it. Maybe one day she will no longer be selfish.

Her boss presses his lips together and raises his eyebrows when she asks for time off. His eyes roll. She wonders if she should have told him the whole truth? How much detail does he need? Does he need to know which ward she'll be visiting and why she doesn't know how much time off she needs? She wonders if she will be fired.

She spends the summer between the end of her first year of uni and the start of her second year in her childhood home. She visits the psych ward every day and fetches new things for her mum. A family photo. A mango. She drives to pick up her sixteen-year-old sister from a friend's house, ferrying her between there and the hospital.

Her grandmother cannot visit often, her cousins are still toddlers, her sister too young to share the load. Her boss gives her one short shift when she returns.

He is nineteen and is expected to step up to his responsibilities. He understands his mum is struggling and he wants to help. He signs his signature and wonders if doing this is enough for her to stop.

His bedroom floor is piled with layers of documents outlining the details of the loans. Different coloured sticky notes let him know where to find the due dates for the personal loan, where to find the extension information for the car loan, and where to find the details to consolidate everything into one loan. He wonders if he will ever see fifty thousand dollars in his name again.

He spends his summer months using his computer programs to set up a timeline of repayments and interest fees. He explains every step to his mum and shows his brother how to edit the information.

He watches the blank faces of his family and wishes his brother didn't have warrants out for his arrest, wishes that his mum's credit rating wasn't so poor.

He hopes her plan works and her credit rating becomes stable once he pays off all of her debts with the loan money. He hopes she will continue giving him access to her banking. Then they can start paying the loan back all together.

He doesn't know that he will be the only one to ever make a repayment.

They have been together for nearly a year and he spins the EFTPOS card between the fingers on one hand while the other hand types a text. He deletes it and sighs.

'Let me help you word it,' she offers and he shrugs. She takes his phone. 'I think if you are as firm as possible, she might realise you mean it this time. And if you tell her what it's like for you when this happens, she might realise that she needs to take you into account.' She types quickly and then hands him back his phone.

He reads it and quickly presses send. He slaps his forehead with the card absent-mindedly, hard enough for the grooves on the card spelling his mother's name to leave small indentations in his skin like reverse Braille.

Hours later his mother throws his bedroom door open. They stay seated on his bed. His mother's eyes are wide as she shouts about being a grown woman who should be able to do whatever she wants with her own money. His mother tells him he's ridiculous.

He trembles and she stands up. She glares at his mother, placing her body in front of his so his mother cannot reach him.

'Stop it. You need to treat him better.'

His mother leaves, slamming the door.

He stands up. 'Thank you,' he says.

'You need to accept that she isn't going to change. You need to open your eyes. And you need to get out.'

Water collects in his eyes and she wraps her arms around him and doesn't let go.

She is twenty and knows right from wrong. She knows she has to do what is the right thing for someone else even when it is the wrong thing for her. Her grandmother says it might be nice, that really it's the right thing to do, if she helps out. It is decided before she can open her mouth.

She visits her seventeen-year-old sister in the Royal Children's Hospital's teenage psychiatric high dependency locked ward. The walls are not white.

She listens to nurses speak about diagnoses and medication and appointments. She keeps a record in her mind of everything they say; she knows her mother will soon be in the adult psychiatric ward in another hospital in another town.

At the end of visiting hours, she blocks out her sister's voice begging to be taken home while her mother pleads with her sister to take a deep breath.

A nurse approaches and asks if she is okay. She has no answer. No one has ever asked her that before.

He is twenty and knows he needs to try harder. He knows he cannot let them down. He wonders why they let him down.

He asks his manager and the second in charge and the store manager. He needs as many shifts as possible. He's not after overtime, just any kind of shift he can get. When his brother's girlfriend moved in he was polite and kind and silently wary. Now his brother has stopped going to his job. He's stopped contributing to buying their groceries.

When his mother had a new excuse for being unable to pay the rent he didn't realise it was an excuse. They'd been doing okay. But then she used the same excuse the next month.

As he works an extra shift, he mentally calculates how long he can keep paying all of the rent, plus the bills with the increase for his brother's girlfriend's usage, as well as all loan repayments, and for four people's worth of groceries.

When he undresses to go to bed at home, he wonders if he somehow managed to stretch his button-up shirt. It is too big for him.

They've been together for over a year and she taps her fingers along the steering wheel as they wait at a red light. She drives through the car park slowly and selects a space in the very back corner. It means they will have to walk a long way; it means she can delay it for just a little longer.

He reaches out and takes hold of her hand as they make their way through the car park. He rubs his thumb in slow circles on her palm. When she stops at the hospital entrance he waits beside her.

'Are you okay?' he murmurs.

She shrugs and takes a deep breath. He squeezes her hand and she leads him to the reception area, grimacing when the nurse asks him to empty his pockets. But he does so without fuss, offering her a small smile. The nurse announces that they are clear to go in and she opens her mouth to warn him. But what can she say? How do you warn a person who is about to enter an adult psychiatric ward for the first time?

He enters before her and accepts the hug her mother throws at him. He keeps hold of her hand as her mother then snatches her up like a mother lion scooping up her cub. He doesn't let go of her hand the entire time.

When they settle back into the car after the visit she stays still for a moment. She turns to him. 'Thank you for coming with me. No one has ever been there for me before, when I've visited.'

'You don't ever have to visit alone again if you don't want to.' He holds both of her hands in his. 'I was thinking about what you said,' he says. 'I want out, I want to get away from my mum. So I was wondering,' he takes a deep breath. 'I'd like to start talking about us moving in together.'

She can't stop the smile from taking over her face. She takes a moment to let it sink in that, with each other, they are no longer alone.

LBD Widow

Zhiling Gao

The first thing you should know about me is that I am a good wife, to every husband of mine. I loved all of them very much – some to death, you may say.

My first husband was a burly Italian, and loved his pasta. His nonna taught me a few of his favourite dishes: spaghetti al pomodoro, fettuccine al carbonara and cannelloni, smothered with oodles of love and butter. After eight years, his arms looked like two barrels, couldn't touch his portly frame. His thick neck worried me a great deal. But a heart vessel burst before his neck swallowed his head. I cried and cried inside the BMW that his papa had bought for him just before the incident.

My second husband always wore Hugo Boss when he entered the courthouse. He said he won more cases in this dark suit. I loved him to bits when I moved into his mini manor in Kew. I shovelled abundant love into his stomach by learning how to make a nice big, fat, juicy steak, perfectly seared brown on the outside.

The trick is the sauces: béarnaise, peppercorn and mushroom gravy, with extra butter and cream. They were to die for, as he had put it, swirling the tulip-shaped glass with a large bottom, looking into the full-bodied red. I would sit across the table, showing my provocative décolletage to the best advantage, smiling and chatting about my day of shopping. He cut the steak into a smaller piece before relishing it, dabbing his mouth with a napkin.

'You are sadistically beautiful,' he would say. By then, his heaving bloated belly had done away with his excellent manner and charm. My spirits were flying high, watching him cutting into the slab of meat with his baby carrot-sized fingers.

The six-o'clock bulletin brought the terrible news: 'A defence lawyer tripped, walking down the steps outside the Magistrate Court with his client.'

I rushed to the Alfred Hospital. The surgeon came out, gloomy faced. 'It was his heart.' I collapsed into his arms that were soft, warm and affectionate. His gentle, slender fingers pressed into the small of my back. I looked up at his pale face and he sniffed down at my chest. There were welding sparks. My Tom Ford scent did its best.

I think you know who my third husband is. I moved into his French Provincial house in Armadale. A Lamborghini with my personalised number plate is parked in the garage. Every morning I break into a wry smile, having his egg and bacon ready and dressing myself for the day.

'I love you in your little black dress,' he said as he crumpled up a few pieces of tissue paper, which looked like a dying dove inside his progressively chubby hand, and wiped fat dripping out of his mouth. 'I'm sorry, I have to work. Have fun at the Derby Day lunch with the ladies.'

I cut in a beam of contentment, walking him to his Mercedes-Benz with white flower fascinator on my large bouncy curls and swaying hips.

At the race three – twelve o'clock exact – the miniature humans bent forward on galloping horses emerged on the track towards us. The delightful ladies and I craned forward and cheered for our own horses, with Moet bubbling at our cherry-red lips and Hollywood teeth. The race caller's voice was rushing with gusto. 'Feh Tarse comes the second. Is Bee Gboob, Bee Gboob came first!'

'I won! I won!' I screamed, stretching my arms up. My black Gucci clutch shook in my right hand.

My iPhone bobbed inside the clutch as if the smartphone was having a seizure.

'It's your husband,' said the nurse at the other end. 'He had a stroke.'

Author Bios

Dominique Carla Davidson is a long time horror fan who lives an active life in a bayside suburb of Melbourne. She is a medical scientist by profession and has recently diversified into the world of dermatoscopy. In her spare time she enjoys working out, swimming, and writing. Dominique's publishing history is unremarkable; a short story in the 2018 Trickster's Treats #2, and a short story in Midnight Echo, the magazine of the Australasian Horror Writers Association. *Marissa's Present* is a story that was inspired by the workplace and has been drafted and re-drafted many times before finding a home.

Odette Des Forges is a Brisbane-based writer. She worked in the travel industry for several years before returning to university to do her Master of Creative Writing. Her work has featured in the *Flight Centre Travel Mag*, *Womankind Magazine*, *In Bloom*, and *The Jacaranda Journal*. She's currently working on the second draft of a novel and there's a lot of coffee drinking and staring into space going on. In her spare time, Odette is an amateur circus artist and co-created a triple trapeze group called the Sisters of Sia.

Samuel Elliott is a Sydney-based writer and interviewer. In addition to finishing his latest historical fiction novel. he also hosts *'The Write Way'* podcast program. All episodes are available on Spotify.

Zhiling Gao is a Melbourne-based legal interpreter, language teacher and writer. Her childhood and early adult years were spent in Inner Mongolia, China. Her short story *Mao's Mango Parade* was awarded the Victorian Writers Centre's Grace Marion Wilson prize, and was published in Eureka Street online magazine. She has a memoir-in-progress *A Little Bag of Power,* which chronicles her experiences growing up during the tumultuous years of Mao's Cultural Revolution. She was awarded a Varuna Publishers'

Fellowship and Asialink Writer's Residency in China.

Jamisyn Gleeson is studying a Master of Creative Writing, Publishing and Editing at the University of Melbourne. She has been published by *Voiceworks* and *Room Magazine* and can usually be found drinking her body weight in coffee and talking about the importance of the Oxford comma.

Rebecca Howden is a Melbourne-based writer. By day she works in content strategy and writes about health; by night she writes stories about obsession, desires and making bad decisions (not at all inspired by experience, obviously). When she's not doing either of those things, you'll find her reading, running along the river, doing yoga (ungracefully), or curling up with her big black cat, Gatsby.

Danielle Hughes lives in the South Eastern suburbs of Melbourne and is a busy mum of four, married to the lovely Derek. With a passion for writing fantasy, Danielle's dream is to successfully self-publish, with the first book in a middle-grade trilogy coming soon.

Melanie Hutchinson is an emerging writer, currently studying for her Masters degree in Creative Writing at Deakin University. When not writing,

Melanie is a violinist masquerading as a technology lawyer. Born and raised in Australia, Melanie has enjoyed several years living in Asia and Europe and traveling the globe. Now she is happily settled in Ngunnawal country with her husband and daughter and two cats.

James Karantonis is a provisional psychologist and postdoctoral researcher from Melbourne, Australia, who has found solace in creative writing. As an escape from reality, a form of expression, and a reliable means of procrastination, James has enjoyed writing short stories, which can be found on his website. He spends his days dreaming about being a science fiction author, and his nights protecting his tomato plants from the local possums.

Linda Kemp is a freelance writer and editor who lives in Melbourne with her husband, three children, and a lazy cat. Linda holds a BA in Professional and Creative Writing, and Honours in Creative Writing, both from Deakin University. Her work, *Moments and Memories*, was published in the 2019 Newcastle Short Story Award anthology. She daily attempts to balance her work and family commitments with writing her first novel, *Blood and Fire*.

Kate Welsh grew up in the homelands of Thomas Hardy in the beautiful and wild Dorset, UK. Inspired by nature and the fragility of human existence, Kate loves to write about the darker side of humanity. Since migrating to Australia, she has worked in the criminal justice system, and uses this to frame her writings about the shadows within our community. Kate enjoys escaping to the beautiful bushlands of Victoria to incorporate our magical and ancient environment within her stories.

Erin McWhinney is a writer and editor based in Melbourne's north. She works in educational publishing and as a freelance editor. Her writing has been published in *Veronica Literary Journal* and Melbourne Polytechnic anthologies *The Last Word* and *INfusion*.

Andrew Nest is an English teacher living in Melbourne. The multiple effects of the coronavirus influenced his writing in 2020. His writing output is the opposite of prolific because of the time he spends obsessively editing the same piece! Pursuits that contribute to his writing include world travel, running, hiking, family, language itself and his emotional convictions.

Laura Pettenuzzo (she/her) lives on Wurundjeri country and is an avid reader and writer. She has a book blog (Laura's Adventures in Literature) and is part of Express Media's Left to Write program for 2021. Laura has been published in OzKids in Print, and Melbourne University's *Antithesis*. As a young woman with cerebral palsy, Laura is passionate about accessibility and is a Plain and Easy English content writer.

Mark Phillips has worked as a journalist and communications professional and writes short stories and non-fiction at a cramped and messy desk in Brunswick. He is the author of *Radio City: the first 30 years of 3RRR-FM* (Vulgar Press, 2006). He has been shortlisted for the 2017 Overland Fair Australia short story prize, and longlisted for 2018 Peter Carey Short Story prize and the 2020 Untitled short story prize. He was most recently published in *On The Street: a Melbourne anthology* (Quiet Corner Publishing, 2020) and in *Lockdown: Melbourne Writers' Group and friends respond to isolation in 2020* (MWG, 2020).

Zachary Pryor (him/he) is an emerging New Zealand writer living in Melbourne on Wurundjeri land. He writes short stories, essays, and flash fiction, along with several half-finished novels.

Author Bios

CJ Quince is a regional Queenslander who spent one too many summers sweltering in Brisbane whilst visiting family. He grew up loving fiction but found it hard to encounter Australian based work that wasn't about droving. C.J. currently resides in Toowoomba with his wife and zero poultry. He spends his spare time writing highfalutin science fiction stories that no one reads.

Justine Stella has a Master of Arts in Writing and Literature from Deakin University. She draws from her experiences to write pieces that hopefully help readers feel like they are not alone.

Jessica L Wilkinson has published three poetic biographies: *Marionette: A Biography of Miss Marion Davies* (2012); *Suite for Percy Grainger* (2014) and *Music Made Visible: A Biography of George Balanchine* (2019), each with Vagabond Press. She is the founder/managing editor of *Rabbit: a journal for nonfiction poetry* and of the offshoot Rabbit Poets Series. She co-edited *Contemporary Australian Feminist Poetry* (Hunter Publishers, 2016) and is an Associate Professor in Creative Writing at RMIT University, Melbourne.

Beau Windon writes quirky stories about quirky people. In 2020 he was selected for the EWF At Home Residency program and was awarded a Varuna Fellowship for 2021. He graduated with an Associate Degree of Professional Writing and Editing from RMIT in 2019 and is currently enrolled in their Bachelor of Creative Writing. You can follow him on social media @WhoIsBeauWindon where he regularly posts madcap ramblings and then anxiously deletes them moments later.

CPSIA information can be obtained
at www.ICGtesting.com
Printed in the USA
BVHW081611060421
604325BV00005B/359